C++ Primer for Non C Programmers

Other McGraw-Hill Titles of Interest

To order or receive additional information on these or any other McGraw-Hill titles, in the United States please call 1-800-822-8158. In other countries, contact your local McGraw-Hill representative.

BC15XXA

C++ Primer for Non C Programmers

Saba Zamir

McGraw-Hill, Inc.

New York   San Francisco   Washington, D.C.   Auckland   Bogotá
Caracas   Lisbon   London   Madrid   Mexico City   Milan
Montreal   New Delhi   San Juan   Singapore
Sydney   Tokyo   Toronto

Library of Congress Cataloging-in-Publication Data

Zamir, Saba, 1959–
    C++ primer for non C programmers / Saba Zamir.
       p.   cm. — (J. Ranade workstation series)
    Includes index.
    ISBN 0-07-072704-X
    1. C++ (Computer program language) I. Title. II. Series
QA76.73.C153Z36 1995
005.13′3—dc20   95-10870
                                                    CIP

1 2 3 4 5 6 7 8 9 0 AGM/AGM 9 0 0 9 8 7 6 5

ISBN 0-07-072704-X

The sponsoring editor for this book was Jerry Papke, the editing supervisor was Bernard Onken, and the production supervisor was Suzanne W. B. Rapcavage.

Printed and bound by Quebecor.

McGraw-Hill books are available at special quantity discounts to use as premiums and sales promotions, or for use in corporate training programs. For more information, please write to the Director of Special Sales, McGraw-Hill, Inc., 11 West 19th Street, New York, NY 10011. Or contact your local bookstore.

This book is printed on acid-free paper.

Table of Contents

PART 2   THE POWER OF C++

To my husband David,

Starting with 'Wish You Were Here' at 21,
And then came the rides to Rockaway,
the Ritchie Blackmore concerts,
the scuba and the ocean,
the trips to Tom's hideaway in Boston,
Richad,
and now Aemin is on her way!
It's been quite a trip!!

Saba Zamir

Preface

C++ is one of the hottest software development platforms of the nineties. This is a direct consequence of the fact that C++ is an object-oriented programming language, and object oriented analysis and design concepts are now gaining ground as one of the most sought after methodologies.

C++ can be considered a natural product of C. It is derived from C, but contains additional features that make it a more powerful language than C. As C++ gained more popularity, the natural migration of programmers that ventured into this arena was comprised of C programmers.

However, programming in C++ presents a unique challenge. It requires a new way of thinking and an object-oriented approach which, unlike C, is non-procedural. In order for programmers to derive benefit from the true powers that C++ has to offer, it was necessary for them to abondon their traditional procedural mode of thinking and instead apply what is called a *modular* approach to their program design. For this reason, it would not be a misnomer to state that it is now no longer necessary, or even desirable, for C++ programmers to be familiar with C.

In addition to this, another significant change started taking place in our fast-paced world. This was the increasing retirement of mainframes, in favor of on-line relational database management systems. The front ends of these systems are increasingly being developed in object-oriented languages such as C++.

Thus, with the passage of time, there are now a new wave of professionals who are attempting to master C++. These people do not know C, or are inherently unfamiliar with it. However, they are expected to learn C++, in order to be competitive in their field.

This book is written specifically for people who fall into one of the categories just described. This book is designed to teach C++ to you even if you have no knowledge, or just a passing familiarity, with C. It will teach C++ as quickly and effortlessly as possible.

WHO THIS BOOK IS FOR

This book is for anyone who needs to learn C++ and knows nothing whatsoever about this language, *or C*. The book can also be used by those who are somewhat familiar with C or C++, and wish to gain a better understanding of its features and concepts. There are no prerequisites for this book, although it is assumed that you have a general understanding of computers.

This book can also be used by students, and it may be used as a textbook for introductory courses in C++.

A WORD ON THE STYLE

This book has been written in such a way that you don't even have to key in a program and see it run, in order to understand the language. This is because sample code is immediately followed by its output, and then a thorough explanation that leaves nothing to the imagination! A hundred plus examples are used to explain each feature of the language. Generally speaking, each example is designed to explain one feature of the language and one feature only. This is so that you can completely and thoroughly understand each feature described, without confusing it with the functionality of another, before reading about the next.

Also, since our lives become more busy and hectic each day, this book is written in such a way that you can practically breeze through it, and yet understand what you are reading.

You will find learning C++ to be a pleasant and painless undertaking!

WHAT IS INCLUDED

Part 1 discusses the basics of programming and C++. It contains discussions on data types, operators, expressions, control structures, and other data constructs in C++. You will feel comfortable with C++ terminology, rules, and constructs by the time you conclude Part 1.

Part 2 describes those features of C++ that make it the unique and powerful language that it is. Classes, derived classes, virtual functions, polymorphism, and operator overloading are explained. There will be no mystery associated with these catch-words by the time you conclude Part 2 of this book.

FINAL WORD

After reading this book, you will find that the difficulty and mystery associated with C++ will be a thing of the past. You will be able to write complex C++ programs, and, more importantly, you will be able to *think object-oriented*. You will understand the importance of the statement just made as you read through this book.

By the way, it should take you no more than one hour to completely understand a chapter. So it should take you less than 24 hours to finish this book! Go for it!

Acknowledgments

Thanks are owed to Gerry Papke, sponsoring editor, and Bernie Onken, editing supervisor, for expediting publication of this book. I can not forget to thank Jay Ranade for finding time to discuss important matters regarding this book, despite his all-too-busy schedule. Thanks are also owed to Nichola Hoffman for her valuable advise (and good company), and Tom Kozak, for providing good cheer whenever I needed it at Moody's. I can not forget to thank Tom Lorenzo for those great getaways in sleepy Burlington!

I thank my mother (Ammi), father (Abjani), and aunt (Khala Jaan) for always being there for me. I thank my son Richad for bringing so much joy to my life. Finally, I would like to thank my unborn child (unborn as of this writing), who I can not quite feel just as yet, but anticipate and count the days.

Saba Zamir

C++ Basics

Thinking
Object Oriented!

1.1 INTRODUCTION

Object Oriented has become one of the key catch-words of the 90's. In its simplest form, the whole idea behind object-oriented design could be expressed as building general solutions for a specific problem, and then customizing these solutions to meet specific needs. The advantages inherent in this kind of design are:

- The ability to reuse what someone else may have designed and written, without extensive re-testing

- The ability to derive new solutions from the basic generalized solution

- The ability to build a system which is *modular* in design.

There are several analogies that can help you understand the concept of a modular system. Consider a *modular couch*. These couches are designed and built in such a way one or more pieces can be added to or taken away from the main couch, based on specific needs, without destroying the functionality or aesthetic value inherent in the design. Consider a *modular home*. These homes are designed in such a way that they can be easily expanded without any major changes to the basic structure of the house. A modular system is similar to the anlogies just presented. It consists of a solid foundation which contains the basic functionality of the system. This foundation is the building block of the remaining system. It can be easily expanded, and new functionalities can be derived from the foundation, without extensive retesting or coding.

The main disadvantage (if you can call it that!) of an object-oriented system is being unable to correctly design a general enough solution that will form the foundation of the system.   Thus, a *long-term view* of the system is essential to building a powerful, useful object-oriented system.

C++ is an object-oriented programming language. However, the fact of the matter is, C++ is nothing more than a procedural language, *unless the system has been designed using object-oriented techniques*. You have to *think object oriented*, in order to bring C++ to life. You have to take the time to think, and think hard, about the design of the system, its foundation, and the solutions that are expected to be derived from its foundation, before you write a single line of code. Unless you think object oriented and modular, C++ is a powerful tool which is entirely useless since it is not being used correctly. This chapter is designed to help you *know how to think, before you start to code*!

1.2 ABSTRACTION

Abstraction lies at the very core of object-oriented design. The art of abstraction lies in being able to concentrate on those features of a system that will formulate the building blocks of everything else that will ensue. Although it is a suprisingly simple concept to understand, it would suprise you to know how infrequently this method is used when it comes to designing anything. In this chapter, we will present a very simplified design of a very complex system. Our objective is to illustrate how complex problems are best analyzed when they are broken down into their simplest components, and how easy it is to build and modify a system that has been carefully analyzed and created in a modular fashion.

Please note that in the interest of simplicity, we will take into consideration only the most generalized features of this system.

1.3 DESIGNING A TELECOMMUNICATIONS SYSTEM

When you pick up the telephone and call someone, a connection is made between yourself and the calling party. In the simplest terms, this is a connection between two points. Your goal is to design a system that captures this connection.

Of course, life is never as simple as a direct connection between two points! We are going to add quite a few more complexities to this system. An example is the best way to explain the whole scenario.

Assume that you wish to place a call to Nichola. Your call can be routed in several different ways:

- You may be lucky enough to have a direct *hotline* to Nichola. In this case, the call would traverse a direct connection like this:

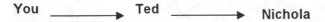

You ⟶ **Nichola**
(no problem)

- Your call may have to be routed to a line that travels through a different location that ultimately leads to Nichola's line, like this:

You ⟶ **Ted** ⟶ **Nichola**

In this scenario, you have a direct line to Ted, and Ted has a direct line to Nichola. In order to reach Nichola, you have to go through Ted's line.

- What happens if Ted's line is busy and you cannot pass through it to reach Nichola? Well, that is the next level of complexity that has to be taken into consideration. It will be necessary for your call to be routed through yet another alternate route that would bypass Ted's line but still lead you to Nichola. This is how the route would look:

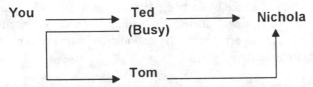

You ⟶ **Ted** ⟶ **Nichola**
(Busy)

Tom

- And now, the final level of complexity. In the real world, the different *links* that we have been talking about (You, Ted, Tom, Nichola) are actually physical hard wired machines. These machines are programmed in such a way that they can accept certain types of incoming phone calls, and redirect them to their destination. Logic is programmed into these machines, (we will refer to these machines as *devices* from now on), so that they can understand the *type* of calls that are directed to them. However, if these calls are of a different type, these devices will not know how to handle them, and therefore reject them. Speaking in technical terms, different types of devices are capable of understanding different types of *protocols*. If the logistics of a phone call does not adhere to a protocol that that device is capable of understanding, then that call will be rejected.

Thus, as a call is routed, it will be necessary to identify the nature of the device that it is expected to traverse through, to ensure that that machine is actually capable of handling and routing this call.

1.4 RETHINKING THE SYSTEM

If you take a moment to reread the previous paragraph, you will find the following issues that need to be addressed in your design of the system:

- How to capture a connection between two points, which may or may not be adjacent to each other

- How to capture the behavior of different devices, which are used to formulate the connection

- How to reroute the call to a different device, if the logical connection that would have been chosen under normal circumstances is not available

Once the main issues that have to be addressed have been listed, the next task is to concentrate on the *essential characteristics* of the different types of objects that will be formulated to implement this system. We try to simplify the complexity of the issues just presented, and this is the result:

- The simplest connection between two points is the one in which they are adjacent to each other, thereby allowing a direct connection between them. An *object* has to be formulated that captures the essence of this connection.

- All devices are ultimately required to implement one main function: the forwarding of a call to the next point. Another *object* has to be formulated that captures the essence of this feature of a *basic* device.

- Before a call is routed from one device to another, the first device has to send a message to the next device asking whether it is available to transport a call to the next point. The subsequent device has to send a message back to the calling device with the appropriate answer. If the device is available, the calling device will forward the call to this device. If it is unavailable, the calling device will try to find an alternate path. This could be classified as the *mechanism* by which the objects formulated will communicate with each other.

The simplified generalizations just presented will form the backbone of the entire system. Once a system has been designed that satisifies the requirements listed, it will be robust enough to handle subsequent complexities, as the next section illustrates.

1.5 Building on the Initial Abstractions

We now summarize the results of our analysis. In the previous section, we listed the functionality of two *objects*. In C++, the functionality of an object is represented in what is called a *class*. The class which is used as a building block for other classes is called the *base class*. In the prvious section, we identified two base classes that would formulate the backbone of the system. These two base classes will form the building blocks of all other classes that will be *derived* from them. The specifications for the base classes can be listed as follows:

- A class that captures the rules required to route a call between two adjacent points. We will call this ClassA.

- A class that captures the functionality of the most basic device used to route a call. We will call this ClassB.

In addition to this, we identified the *mechanism* by which objects of these classes will *communicate* with each other, in order to complete the route of a call.

With these basic building blocks, we add to the complexity of the system, and see how well our base classes are designed to handle these situations. Here are the additional features required by the sytem:

- A call can be routed between two points that are not adjacent to each other, but instead are linked via other connections.

We implement this feature of the system by *deriving a class* from ClassA. This derived class will inherit the rules required to formulate a basic one-to-one connection between two points. However, it will contain additional methods that will contain the rules required to formulate a more complex connection.

- Different types of devices can be added to the system, which handle the route of a call in different ways. However, the basic mechanism by which a call is routed will always remain the same.

We implement this feature by deriving classes from ClassB. These derived classes will inherit the functionality of the most basic device. However, unique attributes or methods that distinguish this device from others will be added for each derivation. The mechanism by which the classes will communical with each other has already been identified.

And believe it or not, that's about it. These should be the basic thought patterns you use to analyze and design a complex system. This system will be flexible enough to handle changes in rules required to complete a route or changes in the attributes of devices. These changes would be implemented simply by modifying the applicable code in the derived classes.

The method for each device will be *encapsulated* in its class. If a new device is added to the system which does not have clearly defined attributes, it can utilize the functionality from the main base class. This functionality would be represented through what is called *virtual functions*. These virtual functions would be overridden once the attributes of the new device are made available, through *polymorphism*.

And now we take a breather to emphasize some of the key phrases and words that you should keep at the back of your mind as you read the remainder of this book. These phrases are: *objects*, *classes*, *base classes*, *derived classes*, *virtual functions* and *polymorphism*.

1.6 CONCLUSIONS

Although this is really a very simplified representation of a system that can be incredibly complex, that is the very point we are making. Keep it simple. Try to simplify the complexity of the problem as much as possible, and concentrate on the main features and requirements without getting bogged down in details that are of no significance to the initial design phase. Do not over-design, but *do get to the root of what is to be conveyed by the system*. If you have the ability to analyze and access the required system in this way, you will be suprised at how easily you will be able to build on the strong foundation that you will create. The complexities of a system are a disguise for the underlying simplicity with which it can be created and implemented, given that you take the time to think, and think hard, of how to break up a complex problem into its simplest components. Once this has been achieved, you will be amazed at how easily everything else will fit into place.

If, on the other hand, there is some flaw in your design, you will also be amazed at how the system will tangle you as you attempt to build on it. A good system will enforce the correct rules; a badly designed system will ultimately become so tangled that it is almost impossible to detangle, usually resulting in a complete rewrite.

Although it is not a prerequisite, I suggest that you read this chapter just one more time (nice and slow) before proceeding to Chapter 2. In Chapter 2, we start our discussion of the language itself.

C++ and Programming Basics

2.1 INTRODUCTION

Before a program can be written, a basic understanding of how it can be saved and run on a computer must exist. In this chapter, we will describe what a program is and how it is processed and executed by a computer. Then, we will write and execute a short and simple C++ program.

2.2 WHAT IS PROGRAMMING?

- **A program is a collection of statements written in a language that can be understood by a computer.**

    The proper execution of a program usually results in some kind of output by the computer.

    A C++ program contains references to code that is prewritten for you. This prewritten code is stored in the form of libraries. These libraries are included in your C++ code through special statements.

- **A program is processed by a compiler, a linker, and a loader.**

    These separate entities are nothing more than different types of software that are stored in the computer and used to process your code in specific ways. The ultimate result of all of this processing is the creation of code in a format that can be understood and run by your computer.

The flow of events that occur from start to finish can be categorized as follows:

Step 1	Programmer logs into a computer.
Step 2	Programmer writes a program using their favorite system editor.
Step 3	Programmer saves the program in a file. This is called the source code file.
Step 4	Programmer instructs the computer to compile the source code file by using the appropriate command.

The command used to compile a program varies for each programming language. For example, the command used to compile a C++ program is different from the one that could be used to compile a BASIC program. If you are using a menu-driven system, the process of compiling and running a program would be nothing more than clicking on the appropriate menu choice.

Let's continue to follow the flow of events and pick up from where we left off. This is what happens once the compilation is started.

Step 5	The compiler translates the source code into assembly language format. This is passed along to the computer's assembler.
Step 6	The assembler translates the assembly language code to relocatable object code. This code is now passed onto the linker.
Step 7	The linker links together all support routines that are referenced in the program. These routines could exist in the run-time libraries, or they could be preexisting, precompiled programs that are referenced by your program. Then, the linker produces the final version of the source code, which is called executable code. This code is now passed onto the loader, which executes the program.
Step 8	The program is run.

As you can see, the entire process is quite lengthy. However, these steps are mostly transparent to you as a programmer. The only steps that you are required to implement are:

Step 1	Create a file containing the source code.
Step 2	Type the command that will result in the compilation of the program.
Step 3	Run the program.

We'll continue our discussion with source naming conventions that you should follow when you save your source code file.

2.3 SOURCE CODE NAMING CONVENTIONS

Different operating systems have varying rules for the names of C++ programs. You should consult your system manual for rules that are applicable to your system. Generally speaking, C++ programs are postfixed with ".C". (That's a capital C; if you postfix with ".c", the compiler will think that you are submitting a C program).

2.4 WHICH COMPILER?

All programs in this book have been compiled and run using the Turbo C++ compiler Version 3.1 in a Microsoft Windows environment on an IBM Personal Computer.

Please note that the programs used in this book are portable. As a matter of fact, one of the strengths of C++ is that it is a highly portable language. These programs will compile and execute using any C++ compiler, which may or may not be installed in a Windows environment.

The Borland compiler understands C programs if they are postfixed with a .c, and C++ programs if they are postfixed with a .cpp. We will use this same convention throughout the book. If you are working with some other operating system or compiler, simply refer to the relevant documentation for applicable instructions. More likely than not, the programs will compile and execute exactly as they would on our system. The code and output should remain the same. Although the wording of the error messages may vary if you are using a different compiler, the context of the messages should remain the same.

2.5 CREATION AND EXECUTION OF A PROGRAM

Before a program can be run, it has to be typed using your favorite (or nonfavorite) editor and stored in a file. Once the file has been created, it is compiled, linked, and run, as required by the particular implementation that is being used. Some implementations allow the above steps to be performed by typing commands at the operating system commmand line prompt. Other systems allow the whole process to be implemented via menus and dialog boxes. Our system is completely menu driven, and allows the user to edit, compile, and run programs using dialog boxes within an integrated environment. For all others, simply "compile" and "run" as instructed by your system documentation.

2.6 BORLAND'S C++ 3.1 COMPILER

We will step through the edit, compile, and run process within the Integrated Development Environment that is provided by Borland's Turbo C++ Version 3.1 compiler. You may select options by positioning and clicking the left mouse button. Or you may simply move the arrow keys to highlight the relevant option and press return. We will adopt the latter method. Options may also be selected via their corresponding hot keys, or by typing the letter designating that command.

We begin our discussion by briefly overviewing the *I*ntegrated *D*evelopment *E*nvironment (IDE) which is Borland's Programmers Platform.

2.7 BORLAND'S PROGRAM MANAGER GROUP

Before you can use a compiler, you obviously have to install it on your PC. You will need to execute the INSTALL program that is provided with this compiler to properly load all applicable files onto your machine. This program assumes that you already have Microsoft Windows installed, and that Program Manager will start up when you start up Windows. After successful installation, on exit and reentry into the Windows environment, Borland C++ will automatically create a new Program Manager group which will contain the group of icons that are related to this platform. There are a total of 20 icons here which are grouped together under the heading Borland C++ 3.1. Please refer to Figure 2.1 for a picture of this group.

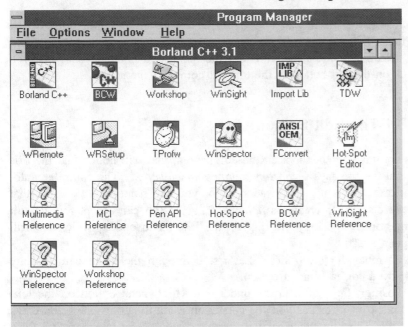

Figure 2.1 Borland C++ 3.1 Icon Group

We will be exploring the menu options available in the Borland C++ for Windows compiler only (second icon from the left). We encourage you to explore the functionality available for the remaining icons; please refer to your C++ documentation for further details.

Position your cursor in the window displayed in Figure 2.1 and double click the left mouse button on the window that says BCW (second icon from the left in the top row). Double click on this now and you will be placed in the IDE platform. This environment contains windows, menus, dialog boxes, a speed bar, scroll bars, and an edit and status line.

2.8 THE IDE PLATFORM

At the top of the IDE screen are the menu options. These will be discussed in detail shortly. Below the menu options is the *Speed Bar*. The speed bar contains a group of icons that provide a shortcut method for implementing frequently used tasks. Position the mouse arrow in any of these icons and a brief description of the functiuonality of that icon will appear in the status field. Please refer to Figure 2.2 for the message that will display (*Display Context Sensitive Help*) when the mouse is positioned on the *?* (Help) icon (the first one on the left).

The arrow keys at the bottom of the screen allow you to scroll the window from left to right. The arrow keys on the right of the screen allow you to scroll the window from top to bottom.

The screen itself can be *maximized* (to cover the entire area of the terminal that you are working on) or *minimized* (changed back to an icon) by selecting the related item from the menu that is displayed when you click on the left button in the top left corner of the screen.

2.8.1 The Edit Screen

As you take another look at the edit screen, you will notice that the title line at the top says *C:\borlandc\bin\noname00.cpp*.   The compiler automatically opens up an edit session for you and names the C++ file that it expects you to create as *noname00.cpp*.   You can accept this default name, or change it by clicking on the File menu option, which we will explain shortly.

So much for the basics! Let's step through the menu bars that are displayed for each menu option.

Position the mouse arrow under *File* (first menu option on the left) and click on it (or position the cursor on it via the arrow keys and press return). The File menu bar will be displayed. Refer to Figure 2.3 for a picture of this menu bar.

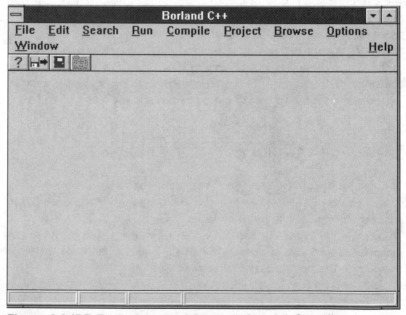

Figure 2.2 IDE Environment of Borland C++ 3.1 Compiler

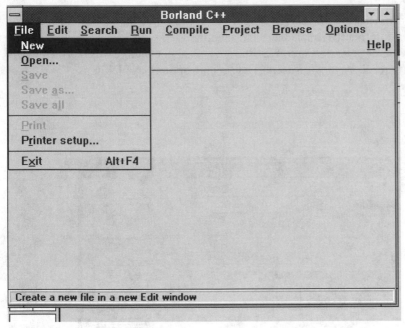

Figure 2.3 File Menu Bar in IDE

You can select any option in the menu bar in one of three ways:

- **Drag the mouse to highlight the chosen option, and then click on it.**

- **Type the letter that is underlined for that menu option, if one is underlined.**

For example, typing *N* will result in your selecting the *New* menu option in the File menu bar.

- **Press the hot key(s) for that option, if one(s) exists.**

For example, pressing the alt key in parallel with function key number 4 will result in the *Exit* option in the File menu bar.

Each menu command that is followed by ellipses (...) implies that a *dialog box* will be activated if this command is chosen. The dialog box will overlay the current window. For example, if you select the *Open* command from the File menu bar, the *Open a File* dialog box will display. Please refer to Figure 2.4 for a picture of this dialog box.

For each dialog box that is opened up, you could type information applicable to that dialog box and then click on *OK* to have the system accept what you just typed. Or, you may click on *Cancel* to have the system discard anything that may have been entered. Click on *Help* for help information related to that window.

Please refer to Figures 2.5 through 2.13 for pictures of the menu bars that are displayed for each of the menu options available.

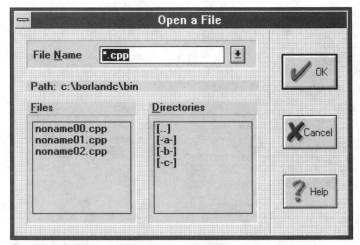

Figure 2.4 Open a File Dialog Box

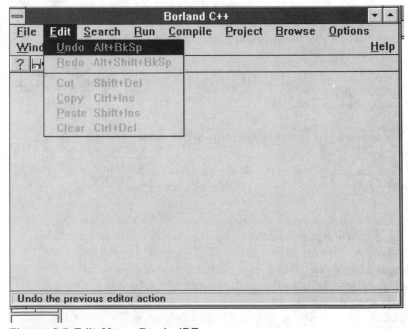

Figure 2.5 Edit Menu Bar in IDE

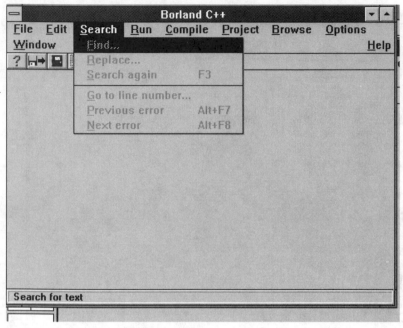

Figure 2.6 Search Menu Bar in IDE

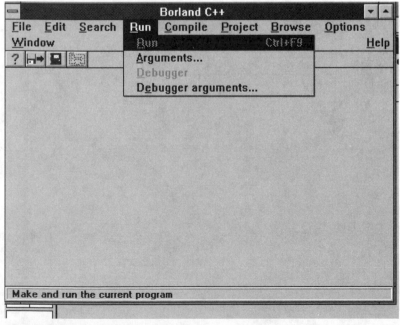

Figure 2.7 Run Menu Bar in IDE

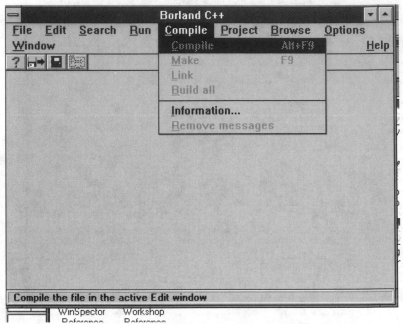

Figure 2.8 Compile Menu Bar in IDE

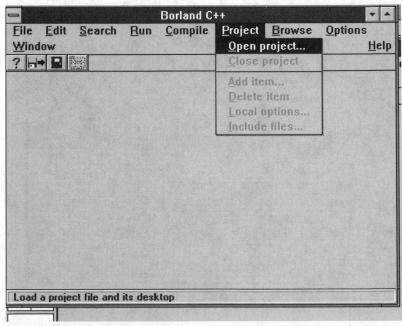

Figure 2.9 Project Menu Bar in IDE

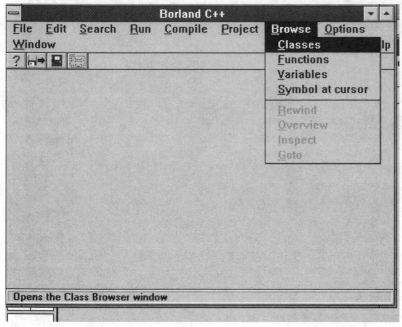

Figure 2.10 Browse Menu Option in IDE

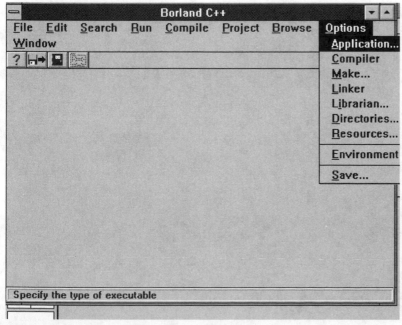

Figure 2.11 Options Menu Bar in IDE

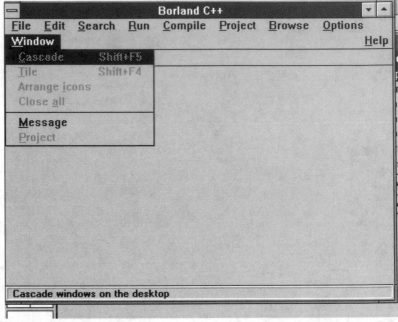

Figure 2.12 Window Menu Bar in IDE

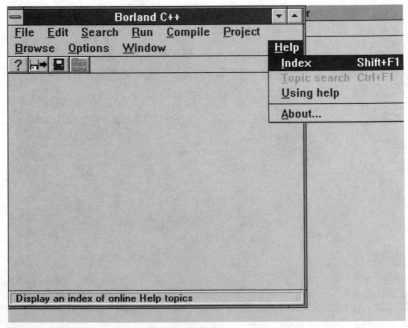

Figure 2.13 Help Menu Bar in IDE

It is beyond the scope of this primer to explain the functionality available in each menu bar, so we refer you to the appropriate system manual for further details. We will, however, describe how you can obtain on-line help for practically any feature.

2.8.2 On-Line Help

Selecting the *Help* menu option will display four commands in its menu bar. If you select *Using Help*, then information similar to what we are about to describe will be displayed. If you select *About...*, then copyright information relating to the product will be displayed. *Topic Search* will allow you to search for help information specific to any topic that you may enter. Let's choose *Index* (shift + F1) and see what happens.

Clicking on *Index* places you in the Borland/Turbo C++ Help window. Please refer to Figure 2.14 for a picture of this screen.

Below the window title is displayed a list of topics. If you position your cursor on any of these topics, the arrow pointer will change into the shape of a hand with a pointed index finger. This implies that further information can be viewed for this topic simply by double clicking on the item that the hand is positioned on. Please refer to Figure 2.15 for the window that was displayed when we double clicked on Dialog Boxes in this window.

You can exit out of any subsequent Help windows by clicking on *Back*. You can scroll forward in the document by clicking on >> and backwards by clicking on <<. You may never have to touch a manual again, because you can scroll through almost the entire documentation available simply by browsing through it on-line.

We now briefly explain how to edit/compile and run a typical C++ program.

2.8.3 The Edit/Compile and Run Process

Choose *File* from the Main Menu Options. You can create a new file, or edit a preexisting one. Choosing *Open* will allow you to edit a preexisting file. The dialog box in Figure 2.4 will be displayed.

We will create a new file. Simply click on *New* in the *File* menu and type in the C++ (or C) program. The Edit menu option provides features designed to edit the program. For the most part, if you make a mistake, simply move the arrow keys to the place where the file has to be edited, use the *Backspace* or *Delete* keys to delete characters, and retype. As you type, it is good practice to save the file frequently.

To save a file, select the *Save as...* command in the *File* menu bar. Clicking on this command will display the Save File dialog As dialog box. Please refer to Figure 2.16 for a picture of this window.

Click on the directory where you wish to save the file. Then, either select the file name from the list that displays under *Files* by clicking on it, or type a new name in File Name. Clicking on *OK* will result in the file being saved.

You may accept the default name (noname001.cpp), or type in the name of your choice as we just indicated. Make sure that C programs are postfixed with a .c, and C++ programs with a .cpp.

Once the file has been saved, compile it by selecting the *Compile* Option from the Main Menu. If there are errors, the compiler will inform you as such. Simply reedit the file, save, and recompile.

Once your program compiles with no errors, select *Run* from the main Menu. Incidentally, if you select *Run* directly after saving a file, this option will compile and execute your program at the same time. The output of a successful run will be displayed on a new screen that will overlay any prior screens.

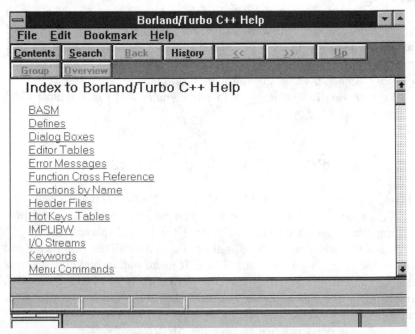

Figure 2.14 Index Sub-Option in the Help Menu Bar

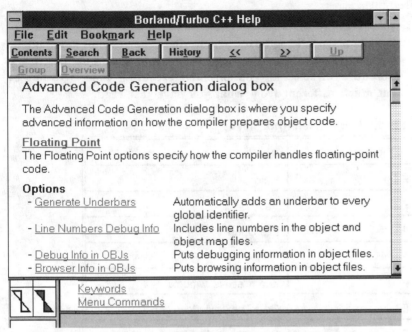

Figure 2.15 Dialog Boxes Help Information

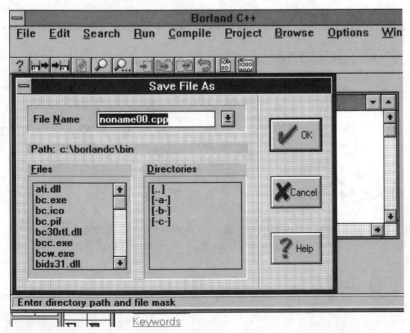

Figure 2.16 Save File As Dialog Box

Table 2.1 lists some commonly used hot keys that allow you to speed up your work.

■ **The menu bar, dialog boxes, windowing schemes, hot keys, and so on, may vary depending on your compiler, but the basic procedure of selecting options and executing them will not be that much different from what you have just read.**

Table 2.1 Some Useful Hot Keys

Hot Key	Result
F1	Help
F2	Save
F3	File/Open
F4	Run
F5	Zoom active window
F6	Go to next window
F10	Go to menu bar

2.9 THE COMPILE PROCESS FOR MENULESS SYSTEMS

Most C++ compilers typically use the command CC to compile the program. The program is run simply by typing its name without its prefix. Here's how:

```
CC source.cpp      <Compiles source code file called source.cpp>
source             <Runs the program>
```

2.10 A C++ PROGRAM

OK. Now that you know how to navigate through the menu system, let's write a small C++ program and run it. Type the following in the edit screen:

```
// test2_1.cpp
#include <iostrem.h>
main()
{
    char name[20];
```

```
    cout << "My name is: ";
    cin >> name;
    cout << name << "\n";
}
```

Save the file by clicking on *Save as...* command in the File menu bar. The Save File As dialog box will display. Click on the directory where you wish to save the file. Then, type `test2_1.cpp` in File Name and click on *OK*. You have just saved the file as test2_1.cpp.

Now, click on *Compile* from the Main Menu. If you typed the program exactly as we display it here, you should receive no errors.

Now select *Run*. A second screen will overlay the existing one. The following will display in this screen:

```
My name is:
```

and the system will wait indefinitely for a response from you. Type your name and hit *Return*. On doing so, whatever you typed will redisplay, and the program will terminate.

2.11 THE EXPLANATION

The first line of the program is:

```
// test2_1.cpp
```

The `//` is used to designate a comment. It can be used anywhere in the program and will be ignored in the compilation process.

The next line is:

```
#include <iostream.h>
```

The `#` symbol followed by the keyword `include` is used to indicate to the compiler that another file is to be included in the compilation of the current program. The file that is to be included is called `iostream.h`. This name is enclosed within angular brackets, implying that this file exists on a specific directory (that is predefined at the time that the compiler is installed).

`iostream.h` contains the standard input and output facilities in C++. In other words, this file has to be included in every program that will perform some kind of input or output. Our program does both, and so we include this file as indicated.

The next line:

```
main()
```

is the main entry point of every C++ program; it must exist. The body of the program is usually contained within the opening and closing curly braces that follow this statement:

```
main()
{
    <body of program>
}
```

The next line:

```
char name[20];
```

is a declaration for a variable that will be used by the program. char implies that this variable is a character data type. name is the name of the variable and its size is 20-bytes long. Thus, the size of a character variable is indicated by the number inside the square brackets.
The next line:

```
cout << "Your name is: ";
```

calls cout. cout is used to output something to standard output. The << symbol is called the put to operator. It is used to output the argument that follows it. In this example, a string of characters is being output. cout is defined as the *standard output stream* in iostream.h. The terminal is usually the standard output stream, and therefore:

```
Your name is:
```

is displayed on the screen.
The next line:

```
cin >> name;
```

calls cin. cin is the standard input stream, also defined in iostream.h. The system waits for you to respond, and stores whatever you enter in the variable called name.
The next line:

```
    cout << name << "\n";
```

outputs whatever was entered back to standard output. Notice the \n at the end of the line. This is an escape character, which results in an automatic carriage return. This is why the cursor will automatically drop to the next line after name is output to the standard output. Notice that this escape character was missing when you typed in your name. This was intentional so that you could type your name next to the prompt.

Each feature in this program will be described in detail later on in the book. For now, we just want you to be able to write, compile, and run a complete C++ program.

A few things worth noting in this program are:

- The existence of the include file

- The existence of main(), and the opening and closing curly braces that follow it

- The declaration of any variables that will be used by the program

- The termination of each statement, except the #include, main() and the curly braces, with a semicolon

2.12 REVIEW

In this chapter we described how a program is written and submitted for compilation and execution. We also described the Borland C++ 3.1 menu-driven system for windows, and the IDE development environment. You now know how to enter a program in this environment, submit it for compilation, and run it. You also know how to access the help files, if necessary.

In the next chapter, we will describe the different types of values that can be handled by a C++ program (called *data*), and the operators used to manipulate these values.

Data Types, Identifers, and Keywords

3.1 INTRODUCTION

The actual values that are manipulated by a program are called data. Data can take various forms; it can consist of numbers or characters. Different types of data are accessed and processed in different ways within C++ programs. This chapter will describe the primary data types.

A program comprises *word-like units* and *white space*. The white space separates the word-like units. The word-like units are known as *tokens*. The combination of tokens and white space makes up a program. This chapter will also describe the different types of tokens that are used to write a C++ program. The specific tokens that will be described are keywords and operators.

3.2 DATA TYPES

The following data types exist in C++:

- integer

- character

- floating point

And now a discussion of the salient features of these data types.

■ **Data types can be constant or variable.**

Constant data cannot be modified through the duration of a program. The values contained in variable data types can be modified as necessary. C++ provides specific notation to indicate these different data types.

In C++ programs, different data types may or may not be required to be declared within the program before they are used.

■ **Constant data types do not have to be declared before they are used.**

On the other hand,

■ **All variable data types must be declared before they are used.**

3.3 IDENTIFIERS AND KEYWORDS

■ **Identifiers are the names that you choose to give to variables and constants (data types), and other entities in a C++ program.**

The first character must be a letter or an underscore. The remainder of the name may contain digits. Letters may be upper- or lowercase. The allowable length of the identifier name varies with different implementations. Our system allows up to 32 characters of significance, but yours may not. Please refer to the documentation for your compiler for rules specific to your implementation.

■ **Data types are declared through *keywords*.**

Keywords are words that you cannot use for your own declarations; they are reserved for C++. Please note that you cannot use reserved words or keywords to name identifiers.

Each data type will now be explained, along with the keywords that are used to declare them in a C++ program.

3.4 INTEGER DATA

■ **An integer is a number that does not have a fractional part. It can be positive or negative.**

Positive integers, such as 32, 45, and 10003, are indicated just as in everyday life. Zero is considered a positive integer. Negative integers, such as -90, and -500, must be preceded with a dash, as indicated.

- **The keyword integer or int is used in the declaration of this data type.**

Here are a few sample declarations:

```
int count, numbers;
```

3.4.1 Short and Long Integers

In order to understand short and long integers, it is worth going into a brief discussion of how a computer stores data. Any kind of information is stored as a binary value in a computer. Binary data is stored in the forms of ones and zeros only. A one or zero is called a *bit*. Four bits make up a *byte*, and four bytes make up a *word*.

The maximum number that can be stored in an integer data type depends on the amount of storage space allocated by a computer. The amount of storage available varies with different computers. For example, one computer may use 16 bits (4 words) to store integer data, while another may use 32 bits (8 words).

When an integer is stored in a computer, the first bit (counting from the left), which is called the zero'th bit, is used to specify whether it is positive or negative.

- **The zero'th bit is set to 1 if it is a negative number; it is set to 0 if it is a positive number.**

The range of numbers that can be stored in a 16-bit computer is from +32,767 to -32,768. The range of numbers that can be stored in a 32-bit computer increases to -2,147,483,648 to 2,147,483,647.

However, if you need to store such a large number in an integer data type in a computer that uses only 16 bits, you can specify *long* integer types.

- **Long integer data types are indicated by prefixing their declaration in a computer with the keyword long. Short integer data types are indicated with the prefix short.**

Here's an example of a long declaration:

```
long int speed_of_light;
```

Long integer types may slow down the execution time of a program.

Short integer data types can be used to speed the execution time of a program. Most computers, however, store short integers in the same amount of storage space as regular integers. Here's how short integers are declared:

```
short int planet_count;
```

- **Long and short declarations can be specified without the keyword int, like this:**

```
long speed_of_light;
short planet_count;
```

3.4.2 Unsigned Integers

- **If you expect that an integer in a program will always be positive, you can precede it with the keyword *unsigned*.**

This will result in an increase in the maximum value that can be stored in it, since the zero'th bit will no longer be required to be used as a sign bit. The range of permissable values that can be stored in unsigned integers increases from -32,768 through +32,767 to 0 through +65,535, for 16-bit computers. Here are a few examples:

```
unsigned large_number;
unsigned int speed;
unsigned long distance;
unsigned short mileage;
```

All of the above variations are acceptable.

3.4.3 Long and Unsigned Constants

Constant values do not change through the duration of a program. Long constants can hold a greater range of values than regular constants.

- **Long constants are indicated as such by suffixing them with l or L, like this:**

```
int 45000l;
int 50000L;
```

Unsigned constants are stored like unsigned integers.

■ **Unsigned integers are indicated as such by suffixing them with** u
or U, **like this:**

```
int 60000u;
int 65535U;
```

3.5 CHARACTER DATA

■ **Character data types are used to represent the alphabet.**

Character data types are actually nothing more than numeric values
that represent characters. These numeric values are based on the ASCII
standard (American Standard Code for Information Interchange.)
According to the ASCII standard, the numeric value of 65 represents a
capital 'A', while 97 represents the small 'a'. Table 3.1 presents the
complete decimal and octal representation of the ASCII code. It is not
necessary for you to learn this code. What is important is that you
understand that each ASCII character is associated with a specific
numeric value.

Table 3.1 The ASCII Code

Dec	Oct	Symb	Dec	Oct	Symb	Dec	Oct	Symb
0	000	^@	43	53	+	86	126	V
1	001	^A	44	54	,	87	127	W
2	002	^B	45	55	-	88	130	X
3	003	^C	46	56	.	89	131	Y
4	004	^D	47	57	/	90	132	Z
5	005	^E	48	60	0	91	133	[
6	006	^F	49	61	1	92	134	\
7	007	^G	50	62	2	93	135	]
8	010	^H	51	63	3	94	136	^
9	011	^I	52	64	4	95	137	_
10	012	^J	53	65	5	96	140	`
11	013	^K	54	66	6	97	141	a
12	014	^L	55	67	7	98	142	b
13	015	^M	56	70	8	99	143	c
14	016	^N	57	71	9	100	144	d

15	017	^O	58	72	:	101	145	e
16	020	^P	59	73	;	102	146	f
17	021	^Q	60	74	<	103	147	g
18	022	^R	61	75	=	104	150	h
19	023	^S	62	76	>	105	151	i
20	024	^T	63	77	?	106	152	j
21	025	^U	64	100	@	107	153	k
22	026	^V	65	101	A	108	154	l
23	027	^W	66	102	B	109	155	m
24	030	^X	67	103	C	110	156	n
25	031	^Y	68	104	D	111	157	o
26	032	^Z	69	105	E	112	160	p
27	033	^[	70	106	F	113	161	q
28	034	^\	71	107	G	114	162	r
29	035	^]	72	110	H	115	163	s
30	036	^^	73	111	I	116	164	t
31	037	^-	74	112	J	117	165	u
32	040	[sp]	75	113	K	118	166	v
33	041	!	76	114	L	119	167	w
34	042	"	77	115	M	120	170	x
35	043	#	78	116	N	121	171	y
36	044	$	79	117	O	122	172	z
37	045	%	80	120	P	123	173	{
38	046	&	81	121	Q	124	174	|
39	047	'	82	122	R	125	175	}
40	050	(	83	123	S	126	176	~
41	051	)	84	124	T	127	177	DEL
42	052	*	85	125	U			

As you glance at this table, notice that there are also numbers for special characters, such as tabs, punctuation marks, control characters (represented by the ^ symbol), and even numbers. Numbers can be represented as integer values (via the keyword int), or they can be specified as characters.

■ **Character data is declared via the keyword** char, **like this:**

char string1, initial;

When a character value is assigned a value, it is enclosed in single quotes, like this:

char yes = 'y'; // character constant yes initialized to y

■ **Character constants can comprise more than one character enclosed within the single quotes. These are the escape sequences, or combinations of characters that have special significance for the compiler.**

Table 3.2 lists the escape sequences that are recognized by our compiler.

Table 3.2 Escape Sequences

Escape sequence	Action taken by the compiler
\a	Rings bell
\b	Backspace
\f	Formfeed
\n	New line character (linefeed)
\r	Carriage return
\t	Tab (horizontol)
\v	Tab (vertical)
\\	Backslash
\'	Single quote
\"	Double quote
\?	Question mark
\nnn	Octal bit pattern, where nnn is an octal number
\xnn	Hexadecimal bit pattern, where xnn is a hexadecimal number

These special characters are used to represent special conditions to the compiler. You have already encountered the use of '\n' in several program.

■ **Special sequences such as these are represented via one or more keystrokes. However, they are considered to be a *single* character by the compiler.**

This particular point will have more significance once we start declaring character strings, later on in the book.

Characters can be initialized to their numeric ASCII equivalent, like this:

```
char A = 65;
```

This would produce the same result as this:

```
char tab = 'A';
```

3.6 FLOATING POINT

- **Floating point data comprise an integer part, a decimal fraction, and optional suffixes.**

This type of data is declared as follows:

```
float half = 0.5;
```

Floating point data can also contain an exponential value and is declared as follows:

```
float big_number = 465.012e3
```

A floating point constant is suffixed with an f or an F:

```
float constant_half = 0.5f;
```

Floating point numbers are usually stored in 32 bits of storage space (assuming a 16-bit computer).

3.7 DOUBLE DATA TYPES

- **A double data type is similar to a float, except that twice as much storage space is reserved for variables and constants of this type.**

Constants such as these can also be suffixed with an l or an L to indicate that they are long.

3.8 CONST DATA TYPES

- **The qualifier const can precede the declaration of any data type to indicate that the value of the variable cannot be changed.**

Thus, const can be used as an alternative way to specify a constant. The following is a const declaration:

```
const ten 10; // ten will always equal the value 10
```

3.9 CASE SENSITIVITY

■ **C++ identifiers are case sensitive.**

A variable declared as follows:

```
int variable;
```

is not the same as this one:

```
int Variable;
```

or this one:

```
int VARIABLE;
```

Here's a small program that illustrates what we have discussed so far:

```
// test3_1.cpp
// iostream.h is necessary for cout
#include <iostream.h>
main()
{
    int   float;   // ERROR - invalid use of keyword as name
    int   sum;     // valid identifier name
    int   Sum;     // valid identifier name
    float = 2;
    Sum = 0;
    sum = 5;
    Sum = sum + float;
    cout << "Sum is  " << Sum << "\n";
}
```

Compiling this program gives several error messages. *Please note that we will list only those messages that are directly related to the error in the program, and will be conforming to this convention throughout the remainder of the book.* Often, other errors are simply offshoots of the real problem, or do not make sense in the context of the actual problem. Here's the message displayed for this program:

```
Error:  Too many types in declaration
```

This is because float is a keyword, and cannot be used as the name of an identifier. This problem can be fixed by changing float to a name that is not a keyword or a reserved word, such as var1. Here's the rewrite of test3_1.cpp:

```
// test3_1.cpp
// iostream.h is necessary for use of cout
#include <iostream.h>
main()
{
    int var1;      // valid identifier name
    int sum;       // valid identifier name
    int Sum;       // valid identifier name

    var1 = 2;
    Sum  = 0;
    sum  = 5;
    Sum = sum + var1;

    cout << "Sum is " << Sum << "\n"
}
```

Compiling and executing the above code result in the correct output:

```
Sum is 7
```

3.10 KEYWORDS REVISITED

The following words cannot be used as identifiers, since they are reserved for use by the C++ compiler:

asm	default	float	new	switch
auto	delete	for	operator	template
break	do	friend	overload	this
case	double	goto	private	typedef
catch	else	if	protected	union
char	enum	inline	public	unsigned
class	extern	int	register	virtual
const		long	return	volatile
continue			short	void
			sizeof	while
			static	
			struct	

3.11 REVIEW

In this chapter, we learned how to declare the basic data types and briefly reviewed how these data types are stored in a computer. Table 3.3 summarizes the storage requirements and range of values for these data types, using a 16-bit computer. Keep in mind that these storage specifications can vary for your computer. If you are working on an IBM or IBM-compatible PC, then the storage specifications will probably be the same.

Table 3.3 Data Types and Storage Requirements

Data type	Declaration in C++	Storage	Permissable values
Integers	int	16 bits	-32,768 to +32,768
Integers, short	short int	16 bits	-32,768 to +32,768
Integers, long	long int	32 bits	-2,147,483,648 to +2,147,483,647
Integers, unsigned	unsigned int	16 bits	0 to 65,535
Integer constants, long	Add suffix l or L	32 bits	-2,147,483,648 to +2,147,483,647
Integer constants, unsigned	Add suffix u or U	16 bits	0 to 65,535
Character	char	8 bits	ASCII code
Float	float	32 bits	3.4×10^{-38} to $3.4 \times 10^{+38}$
Double	double	64 bits	1.7×10^{-308} to $1.7 \times 10^{+308}$
Double, long	Add suffix l or L	80 bits	3.4×10^{-4932} to $1.1 \times 10^{+4932}$

Storage Classes
and Scope

4.1 INTRODUCTION

In the last chapter, we learned the different data types that exist in C++. In this chapter, the storage classes of these types will be discussed.

- A *storage class* implies the location in which the variable will be stored and its duration or lifetime through the execution of the program that contains it.

Tied closely to storage class is *scope*.

- Scope is that part of a program in which the variable is active; that is, it can be accessed.

- A variable's storage class can be implied *explicitly*, by stating it as such, or *implicitly*, by its context.

It defaults to the storage class implied by its context. The following storage classes exist in C++:

```
automatic
static
external
register
```

- Storage classes have *defaults*.

What that means is that if the storage class of a variable is not declared, the compiler believes it to be of the default class that is implied by its context. Subsequent sections in this chapter explain each storage class in detail.

4.2 AUTOMATIC DECLARATIONS

■ **The keyword** auto **is used to declare automatic variables. Variables that are declared without specifiers default to** auto.

Take a look at this code:

```
auto int a;     // automatic variable
char   b;       // automatic variable by default
```

■ **In C++, the scope (duration during which its value is active within a program) of an automatic variable is only for the block, or any blocks within that block, in which it appears.**

Here's an example that illustrates the scope of an automatice variable:

```
// test4_1.cpp

#include <iostream.h>
main()
{
    // i and j are auto variables by default
    int i;
    int j;

    cout << " i in outer block is " << i << "\n";
    cout << " j in outer block is " << j << "\n";
    cout << " k in outer block is " << k << "\n";

    { //    inner block
      int k;       // auto variable by default
      cout << " i in inner block is " << i << "\n";
      cout << " j in inner block is " << j << "\n";
      cout << " k in inner block is " << k << "\n";
    }

    //    outer block again
    cout << " i back in outer block is " << i << "\n";
    cout << " j back in outer block is " << j << "\n";
    cout << " k back in outer block is " << k << "\n";

} // end main()
```

Compiling this program results in the following error messages:

```
Error:   Undefined symbol 'k' in function main()
Error:   Undefined symbol 'k' in function main()
```

This is because the variable k is auto by default. It is declared inside the inner block, and it exists, or can be accessed, only within this block. The compiler does not know the value of k in the outer block, (k is *out of scope* in the outer block), and hence generates error messages. The error can be fixed simply be declaring k in the outer block and deleting its declaration in the inner block. After doing so, recompiling and executing the program gives the following output:

```
i in outer block is 8886
j in outer block is 18
k in outer block is 0
i in inner block is 8886
j in inner block is 18
k in inner block is 0
i back in outer block is 8886
j back in outer block is 18
k back in outer block is 0
```

So where did the values 8886, 18, and 0 magically appear in the variables i, j, and k? Well, in C++, if automatic variables are not initialized within their scope, they contain random or garbage values. If the original declarations of i, j, and k are modified as follows:

```
     .
     .
int i = 1;
int j = 2;
int k = 3;
     .
     .
```

then the output changes to this:

```
i in outer block is  1
j in outer block is  2
k in outer block is  3
i in inner block is  1
j in inner block is  2
k in inner block is  3
i back in outer block is 1
j back in outer block is 2
k back in outer block is 3
```

4.3 STATIC DECLARATIONS

- **Static variables are declared as such by preceding their declaration with the key word *static*.**

Like automatic variables, these variables are also local to the function, block or subsumed blocks in which they exist. However, there is one important difference.

- **Values of static variables persist, or *stick*, even when the variables go out of scope.**

When the program comes back to the same function, processing proceeds with the last values that were stored in them. Also,

- **Static variables in the absence of initializers are automatically initialized to 0 or null.**

Take a look at the following program:

```
// test4_2.cpp

#include <iostream.h>

// function prototype follows
void sum(void);

main()
{
    // j is a static declaration
    static int j;

    sum();
    cout << "Inside main(), j is  " << j << "\n";
    sum();
    cout << "Inside main(), j is  " << j << "\n";
}

void sum(void)
{
    static int j

    j = j+1;
    cout << "Inside sum() j is %d " << j <<  "\n";
}
```

Compiling and running the program result in the following output:

```
Inside sum() j is 1
Inside main(), j is 0
Inside sum() j is 2
Inside main(), j is 0
```

j is declared as a static variable inside the functions main() and sum(). Inside sum(), 1 is added to j, and thus, j is set to 1. Then, processing goes back to main(), and we see that the value of j is 0. This is because the variable j in main() is out of scope in the function sum(). In the absence of explicit initializers, statics are set to 0. Hence, the value 0 is output for the value of j in main(). Next, control is returned to sum(), and here the old value of 1 that was placed in j persists, (because it is static), and now j is set to 2. Inside main(), the value of j is still 0.

In C++, static members of classes have special rules associated with them. These will be discussed in detail when we discuss classes.

4.4 EXTERNAL DECLARATIONS

■ **External variables differ from static and automatic variables in that their scope is *global* instead of local.**

External variables can exist outside or inside functions, and are available to all functions that are within the same file (this is known as *file scope*).

■ **The values of external variables persist, just like statics.**

■ **In the absence of explicit initializers, externals are set to 0 or null.**

Take a look at the following program:

```
// test4_3.cpp
#include <iostream.h>

// i is a global extern declaration
int   i;

// function prototypes follow
void function_1(void);
void function_2(void);

main()
{
    cout << " i inside main() is " << i << "\n";
    function_1();
```

```
}

void function_1(void)
{
   i = i + 1;
   cout << " i inside function_1() is " << i << "\n";
   function_2();
}

void function_2(void)
{
   i = i + 1;
   cout << " i inside function_2() is " << i << "\n";
}
```

Compiling and running this program result in the following output:

```
i inside main() is 0
i inside function_1() is 1
i inside function_2() is 2
```

i outputs as 0 in main(), since it was not explicitly initialized. Inside function_1(), it outputs as 1. There is no need for a declaration of i inside function_1(), since it has been declared globally outside of main(). Inside function_2(), it outputs as 2, since the value set in function_1() persists.

Externals can be declared as extern inside the function in which they are used. The compiler would accept the following change to the original program without any change in output.

```
        .
        .
void function_1(void)
{
   extern int i;
        .
        .
}

void function_2()
{
   extern int i;
        .
        .
}
```

The rule that must be followed is that the extern declaration should be outside and above the function that references it, and within the same source code file. The compiler will generate an error for the following program:

```
// test4_4.cpp
#include <iostream.h>

// i is an external declaration
int i;

main()
{
   i = 5;
   cout << " i is " << i << "\n";
   cout << " j is " << j << "\n";
}

// j is declared after being referenced
int j;

Error:   Undefined symbol 'j' in function main()
```

This problem can be fixed by simply moving the declaration of j next to i. Another fix would be to leave the code the way it was in the original program, and add an extern declaration for both i and j inside main():

```
.
.
int i;
   .
   .
main()
{
   extern int i;
   extern int j;
   .
   .
}

int j;
```

Compiling and running this program would produce the following output:

```
i is 5
j is 0
```

And now, a word of advice. *C++ capitalizes on the concept of privacy of data, and you will learn how in subsequent chapters. We recommend that you use external variables only when absolutely necesary. Since privacy of data is lost, they take up storage space throughout the duration of the program because they are global in scope. In a program of any fair length, it may be hard to keep track of what value is stored in them in different functions at different times.*

4.5 REGISTER DECLARATIONS

Register variables behave like automatic variables in that they are local in their scope. However, when a variable declaration is preceded with the keyword *register*, it means that a request has been made to the compiler to store that variable in a register, if one is available.

■ **Use of register variables can significantly reduce the size of a program and improve its performance, since operations on registers are faster than those performed for variables stored in memory.**

The following are valid register declarations:

```
register int  a;    // register declaration
register char b;    // register declaration
```

The keywords auto and register cannot appear in an external declaration.

4.6 DURATION OF VARIABLES

■ **The duration of a variable is the period of time that a variable is assigned memory.**

As indicated previously,

■ **Static and external storage class variables are assigned memory for the complete duration of the program.**

■ **Auto and register variables are assigned memory while they are within their enclosing block or function.**

■ **You can also dynamically allocate storage to variables via the operators new and delete.**

These operators will be discussed in subsequent chapters. We mention them now so that you know they exist.

4.7 REVIEW

In this chapter, we discussed storage classes. Table 4.1 illustrates the major concepts discussed:

Table 4.1 Storage Classes in C++

Storage class	Scope	Memory allocation	Initialization by compiler
auto	Local to block, subsumed block, or function in which it is declared. Values do not persist.	While in scope	None
static	Local to block, subsumed block, or function in which it is declared. Values persist.	Duration of program	0
extern	Globally available to all functions within the same file, if declared outside and above them. Values persist.	Duration of program	0
register	Local to block, subsumed block, or function in which it is declared. Values do not persist.	While in scope	None

Operators, Precedence, and Associativity

5.1 INTRODUCTION

■ **An operator is a symbol which represents an operation that can be performed on a data value.**

An operator operators on an operand. This operand is a data value, and it can a constant or a variable.

C++ contains a rich set of operators. Some of these operate on one operand, some on two. Some operators are distinct on their own, while some are derived from others. Some of them are even *overloaded*. What this means is that the same operand can imply more than one operation, the compiler understands the correct operation that is to be performed by the context in which it is used.

It is rare to find a program in which all of these operators are used. In this chapter, we will discuss only the most basic ones, which are the arithmetic, assignment, modulus, increment and decrement operators. Almost all programs in C++ reference these operators. The more specialized ones will be discussed in subsequent chapters.

■ **Precedence refers to the order in which operations are carried out in a program.**

One C++ statement can contain multiple operators that perform multiple operations on the data types that they reference. However, these operations have to be performed in some order, or the same statement will produce different results. Just like you use brackets to specify the precedence of operations inside arithmetic operations (the operation inside the bracket is performed before the operation outside of it), the precedence of operations to be performed on a C++ statement are implied by the operators themselves. This chapter will discuss the order of precedence in which operations are performed.

5.2 THE ARITHMETIC, ASSIGNMENT, AND MODULUS OPERATORS

You have already encounterd some of the arithmetic and assignment operators. Here's a simple statement that uses the plus (+) operator:

```
a = 5 + 5;
```

There are three operands in this statement: a, 5, and 5. The first operand is a variable, while the remaining two are constants. The operand on the far left is the one in which the result of the operation is stored. Thus, a receives the result of the operation of adding 5 to 5, which is 10. The plus operator is used to add the operands to the left and right.

Here's a short program that utilizes the remaining math operators:

```
//test5.1.cpp

#include <iostream.h>
main()
{
    int a, b, c, d;

    a = 5 + 3;      // plus operator
    b = a - 2;      // minus operator
    c = a + b;      // plus operator
    d = c / 2;      // divide operator
    e = d * 4;      // multiply operator
    f = e % 5;      // modulus operator

    cout << "a is " << a << "\n";
    cout << "b is " << b << "\n";
    cout << "c is " << c << "\n";
    cout << "d is " << d << "\n";
    cout << "e is " << e << "\n";
    cout << "f is " << f << "\n";
}
```

Compiling and running this program will result in the following output:

```
a is 8
b is 6
c is 14
```

```
d is 7
e is 28
f is 3
```

The output is self-explanatory for all operators but perhaps the last one.

- **The modulus operator is used to acquire the remainder of a division operation, instead of the quotient.**

The contents of e, (i.e., 28) is divided by 5. The quotient, which is 5, is discarded, while the remainder, which is 3, is stored in f.

5.3 THE INCREMENT AND DECREMENT OPERATORS

This statement:

```
a = a + 1;
```

can also be expressed like this:

```
a++;
```

a++ utilizes the use of the increment operator (++). The results of the two statements are identical, a is incremented by 1.

Along the same lines, this statement

```
b = b - 1;
```

can also be expressed like this:

```
b--;
```

b-- utilizes the decrement operator (--).

In the examples above, the increment and decrement operators are used in their suffix positions (i.e., they follow the operand). These operators can also be used in their prefix positions, like this:

```
++a;
--b;
```

There is a difference in the results of the two operations. The difference between them can be understood more easily if another variable is used to store the results of these operations. Assume that a has 10 stored in it. This statement

```
c = a++;
```

will result in 10 being stored in c, and then a is incremented by 1. The end result will be as follows:

Variable	Contents
c	10
a	11

On the other hand, this statement

```
c = ++a;
```

results in a first being incremented by 1, and then c being stored with its new value. The two variables are changed like this:

Variable	Contents
c	11
a	11

Here's the before and after scenario using the decrement operator. Assume that a has 20 stored in it this time:

```
c = b--;
```

The result is:

Variable	Contents
c	20
b	19

Using the prefix position:

```
c = --b;
```

has the following results:

Variable	Contents
c	19
b	19

5.4 COMPOUND OPERATORS

As explained in the previous section, this expression

b = b+1;

can be expressed like this:

b = b++;

C ++ allows us to express the same expression like this as well:

b += 1

The syntax looks like this:

variable operator = expression

This type of sytax can be used with the following operators:

```
=
+=
*=
-=
/=
%=
```

Thus, the expression

a = a * 5;

can also be expressed as

a *= 5;

It can also be used with the bitwise operators, which will be described in detail later in this chapter. These operators are:

```
>>=
<<=
&=
^=
|=
```

5.5 THE LOGICAL AND OPERATOR

■ **The logical AND operator is represented by the symbol &&.**

■ **It is used to perform a logical combination of one or more conditions.**

If the existence of two or more conditions are to be evaluated, they are combined together using &&.

For example, assume the following is to be coded:

If age is less than or equal to 55, and person is in good health, issue life insurance.

If age is less than or equal to 55, and person is in bad health, do not issue life insurance.

If age is greater than 50, do not issue life insurance.

These conditions could be coded using the if statement. (The if statement is discussed in detail in the next chapter.) The logical AND operator can be used to combine these conditions to acquire the required result. Here's the program that does it:

(P.S.: Don't worry if you don't get the complete syntax of the if statement right now! It is fairly intuitive to understand, and we think you'll get the idea anyway.)

```
// test5_2.cpp
#include <iostream.h>

main()
{
    char life_insurance[1];
    char health[1];
    int age = 50;

    health = 'B';

    if (age <= 55 && health == 'G')
        life_insurance = 'Y';
    if (age <= 55 && health == 'B')
        life_insurance = 'N';
    if (age > 55)
        life_insurance = 'N';
    cout << "Life insurance issued: " << life_insurance << "\n";
}
```

The output for this program is:

```
Life insurance issued: N
```

In this program, the necessary variables are declared, and then `health` is initialized to B for *Bad*. The `if` statement is executed three times. In the first statement, the check is that if age is less than or equal to 55 AND health is good, set `life_insurance` to Y for *Yes*. The second if statement says that if age is less than or equal to 55 AND health is B for *Bad*, set `life_insurance` to N for *No*. You should be able to figure out the meaning of the third `if` statement.

Please note that

■ **The && operator is used to combine the two conditions together**

■ **The conditions to the left and right of the && operator must both be true for the complete expression to be evaluated as TRUE (remember, a nonzero value implies TRUE, a zero value implies FALSE).**

5.6 THE LOGICAL OR OPERATOR

■ **The logical OR operator is represented by the ‖ symbol.**

The ‖ evaluates the expressions it combines, just like the AND. The difference is that:

■ **Any one of the conditions can be true, in order for the expression to evaluate as TRUE, not all conditions, like the AND.**

The program in the previous section can be rewritten, using the ‖ operator, like this:

```
// test5_3.cpp
#include <iostream.h>

main()
{
    char life_insurance[1];
    char health[1];
    int age = 50;

    health = 'B';

    if (age <= 55 && health == 'G')
        life_insurance = 'Y';
```

```
if (age <= 55 && health == 'B') || (age > 55)
    life_insurance = 'N';
cout << "Life insurance issued: " << life_insurance << "\n";
}
```

The output for this program is:

```
Life insurance issued: N
```

Notice that the || operator is used to combine the second and third if statements. Thus, if either one of these conditions are true (the one on the left *OR* the one on the right of the || operator), then the expression evaluates as TRUE.

5.7 THE BITWISE OPERATORS

As you already know, four bits make a byte, and four bytes make up a word. A 16-bit computer usually stores a character in one byte of memory and an integer in one word. Floating point numbers are stored in two words, and so on. Whatever the case, data is always stored as a combination of 1's and 0's; this is the machine representation of the data. Sometimes, it is necessary to be able to manipulate data at the bit level. That is, a programmer may wish to change the data stored in a bit, byte, or word, by modifying the 0's and 1's that are used to represent it. This is where bitwise operators come into play.

5.7.1 The Left and Right Bitwise Shift Operators

You have already encountered the use of the *put to* (>>) and get (<<) operators.

- **The << operator is also used to shift data in a word to the left by a specific number of bits.**

- **The >> operator is also used to shift data in a word to the right by a specific number of bits.**

Here's a program that illustrates their use:

```
// test5_4.cpp
#include <iostream.h>
main()
{
```

```
    int age = 6;
    int new_age;

    new_age = age << 4;
    cout << "new_age is: " << new_age "\n';
}
```

The output for this program is:

```
age is 96
```

At the beginning of the program, age is initialized to 6. Take another look at the statement:

```
age << 4;
```

What this does is shift whatever was stored in age left by 4 bits. At the machine level, 6 is represented as follows:

```
0000 0000 0000 0110
```

Four bits are shifted to the left, like this:

```
0000 0000 0110 ...
```

The vacant bits are filled with zeros, like this:

```
0000 0000 0110 0000
```

and the result in the number 96.

The right shift operator (>>) works just like the left shift operator, except, of course, it shifts the bits to the right. Here's test5_4.cpp modified to use the right shift operator instead:

```
// test5_5.cpp
#include <iostream.h>
main()
{
    int age = 6;
    int new_age;

    new_age = age >> 4;
    cout << "new_age is: " << new_age "\n';
}
```

The output for this program is:

```
new_age is 0
```

Once again, the number 6 whose internal representation is:

0000 0000 0000 0110

is shifted right by 4 bits, like this:

... 0000 0000 0000

and the vacant bits are filled in with zeros. Please note that the guarantee of zeros filler bits exists only if the variable being shifted right is unsigned (i.e., always positive.) In summary:

- **The left bitwise operator (<<) is used to shift bits of data to the left.**

- **The vacant bits are filled with zeros.**

- **The right bitwise operator (>>) is used to shift bits of data to the right.**

- **The vacant bits may or may not be filled with zeros. Zeros are guaranteed only if the variable being shifted is unsigned. Sometimes, the sign bit fills in the vacant bits.**

    Please note that:

- **The results of the bitwise operation can be unpredictable if the expression to the right of the operator is negative, or greater than the expression on the left.**

5.7.2 The AND Bitwise Operator

- **The bitwise AND operator is used to find the logical product of two integral operands.**

- **Two bits are ANDed together via the AND operator, represented by the symbol &.**

- **The bitwise AND operator yields a 1 only if the two bits being ANDed are both 1. Otherwise, it yields a 0.**

Thus,

0 & 0 is 0
0 & 1 is 0
1 & 0 is 0
1 & 1 is 1

Here's a concrete example, where the number 128 is ANDed with a negative 97:

$$
\begin{array}{r}
0000\ 0000\ 1000\ 0000 \\
\&\ \underline{1111\ 1111\ 1001\ 1111}\ \text{gives} \\
0000\ 0000\ 1000\ 0000
\end{array}
$$

Thus, the number 128 ANDed with the number -97 yields the number 128.

Here's how the example would look like in C++:

```
// test5_6.cpp
#include <iostream.h>

main()
{
    int a = 128;
    int b = -97;
    int c;

    c = a & b;

    cout << "c is: " << c << "\n";
}
```

The output for this program is:

```
c is 128
```

and should be self-explanatory.

5.7.3 The OR Bitwise Operator

- **The bitwise OR operator is used to find the logical sum of two integral operands.**

- **Two bits are ORed via the | operator.**

- **A bitwise OR yields a zero if both bits are zero. Otherwise, the result is 1.**

Thus,

0 | 0 is 0
0 | 1 is 1
1 | 0 is 1
1 | 1 is 1

Here's the example presented in the previous section using the |
operator:

```
     0000 0000 1000 0000
|    1111 1111 1001 1111  gives
     1111 1111 1001 0000
```

and here's the C++ example:

```
// test5_7.cpp
#include <iostream.h>

main()
{
    int a = 128;
    int b = -97;
    int c;

    c = a | b;

    cout << "c is: " << c << "\n";
}
```

The output is:

```
c is -97
```

5.7.4 The Bitwise XOR Operator

- **The bitwise XOR operator is used to perform an EXCLUSIVE-OR. Two bits are EXCLUSIVE-ORed through the ~ operator.**

In an XOR:

0 ^ 0 is 0
0 ^ 1 is 1
1 ^ 0 is 1
1 ^ 1 is 0

Here's the example from the prior two sections, using the XOR:

```
      0000 0000 1000 0000
  ^   1111 1111 1001 1111   gives
      1111 1111 0001 1111
```

and here's the C++ program:

```cpp
// test5_8.cpp
#include <iostream.h>

main()
{
    int a = 128;
    int b = -97;
    int c;

    c = a ^ b;

    cout << "c is: " << c << "\n";
}
```

The output is:

```
c is -225
```

5.8 THE NEW AND DELETE OPERATORS

The new and delete operators are discussed in greater detail later on in the book, when we discuss constructors and destructors. We present a brief discussion here for the sake of completeness.

■ **The operator new is used to dynamically storage to different data types from the free store or heap.**

The *free store* is a pool of unallocated memory that is provided to the program when it is run. The variable is continued to be allocated space until memory is deallocated via the operator delete.

■ **The delete operator is used to deallocate memory allocated by new.**

Exactly how this works has to do with a *pointer* that is returned by new. The subject of pointers have not been discussed yet; for now, think of a pointer as a number representing a specific location in memory where a variable is stored.

On successful allocation, the new operator returns a pointer to that location in memory. A null pointer is returned on unsuccessful allocation. The operator delete uses the same pointer to deallocate memory when it is invoked.

The use of delete is not mandatory, since memory will obviously be automatically deallocated on termination of the program.

5.9 The sizeof Operator

■ **The sizeof operator is used to return the size of the operand that it is applied to. The size is returned in bytes.**

For example, the following statements

```
char a[1];
sizeof(a);
```

will return 1, which is the size of a. Along the same lines, the following statements:

```
int j;
sizeof (j);
```

will return 2, since an integer is stored in two bytes.

■ **sizeof can be used to return the size of any valid data type.**

5.10 The Conditional or Ternary Operator

■ **This conditional operator is a variant of the if-else statement.**

It is infrequently used, since the if-else is that much more intuitive to use and understand. Although the if-else construct has not been discussed yet (detailed explanations follow in Chapter 6, you'll get the idea of what we mean when you see the pseudo-code), we present an explanation for this operator in this chapter, for the sake of completeness. Here's the syntax:

expr1 ? expr2 : expr3

It is evaluated as follows: If expr1 (expression1) is true, the value returned will be expr2; if expr1 is false, the value returned will be expr3.

This is how this same condition would have been represented using the `if-else` construct:

```
if (expr1 is true)
    do expr2;
else
    do expr3;
```

Here's how a typical statement using this operator would look in C++:

```
a = b ? 2 : 4;
```

This statement is deciphered like this:

if b is true (i.e., equal to a nonzero value), set it equal to 2. If b is false, (i.e., equal to zero), set it equal to 4, and then set a equal to b.

5.11 PRECEDENCE AND ASSOCIATIVITY

- *Precedence* **refers to the order in which operators are evaluated in a statement.**

- *Associativity* **refers to the order in which multiple operators of the same type are evaluated within the same statement.**

- **C++ has a built-in set of rules that dictate the order in which operations are to be evaluated.**

Table 5.1 lists the associativity and precedence of C++ operators. Most of these operators have been explained. The remaining will be explained in subsequent chapters.

- **The order of precedence for each set of operators that appears on one line is from left to right.**

Thus, ( ) and [ ] have the same precedence. These operators will take precedence over the operators in the subsequent lines, such as ! and ~. However, if both ( ) and [ ] are encountered in one statement, then ( ) will be evaluated before [ ].
Now did you ever wonder what precedence will be applied if the same operator occurs multiple times within the same statement? Take a look at this example:

Table 5.1 Associativity and Precedence of C++ Operators

Operators	Associativity
() [] -> :: .	Left to right
! ~ - ++ -- & *	Right to left
sizeof new delete .* -> / %	Left to right
+ -	Left to right
<< >>	Left to right
< <= > >=	Left to right
== !=	Left to right
&	Left to right
^	Left to right
|	Left to right
&&	Left to right
||	Left to right
? conditional operator	Right to left
= += /= %= += -=	Right to left
&= ^= |= ,	Left to right

```
a = b = 5 + 1;
```

Will b be assigned to 5, and a be assigned to b+1, i.e., 6? Or will 6 be assigned to b first, and then this value stored in a? In the first case, a will contain 5, and b will have 6 stored in it. In the second case, both a and b will contain 6.

Well, it may suprise you to know that

■ **C++ does not have a set of rules that evaluate the precedence of the same operator which occurs multiple times within a statement.**

In cases such as these, alway use parentheses to specify the order that you want, in this way you avoid unpredictable results. Thus, the expression that will result in a being assigned 5 and b 6 will be coded like this:

```
a = (b = 5) + 1;
```

The location of parentheses in the second case will change as follows:

```
a = b = (5 + 1);
```

5.12 REVIEW

In this chapter, we discussed precedence and associativity of operators. Precedence refers to the order in which operations are carried out in a program, while associativity refers to the order in which multiple operators of the same type are evaluated within the same statement. We described the usage of the arithmetic, assignment, modulus, increment, decrement, logical AND and OR, bitwise, new, delete, sizeof, and conditional operators. We also desribed how compound operators work.

Control Structures

6.1 Introduction

If you understood the contents of the last chapter, then you should read this one. If you did not understand Chapter 5, then you should read that chapter again before continuing with this one.

What we just said is an illustration of conditional logic, utilizing an *if* statement. A computer program utilizes all kinds of conditional logic; if this condition is true, do this; otherwise do this.

- **Control structures enable us to specify the logic or flow of control in a program.**

In this chapter, the following control structure will be explained:

The `if` and `if-else` statements
The `while` statement
The `do-while` statement
The `for` statement
The `switch-case` construct

6.2 The `if` and `if-else` Statements

The `if` statement is conditional execution in its simplest form. The logic can be translated into pseudo-code like this:

```
if (this condition is true)
    {
    do this;
    and this;
    }
```

Notice that parentheses enclose the condition that is being tested, and braces enclose the set of statements that are to be performed if that condition is true. If only one statement is performed, then the braces are not required. A semicolon, as usual, terminates each statement.

So what happens if this condition is not true? The else statement can be appended to the if statement, like this:

```
if (this condition is true)
    {
    do this;
    and this;
    }
else
    {
    do this;
    and this;
    }
```

So how do we state a condition, and how is it evaluated to be true or false?

- **Conditions are represented through the use of C++ relational operators.**

Here's a list of them and what they mean:

Table 6.1 Relational Operators in C++

Operator	Meaning
==	Operand on the left is equal to the operand on the right
!=	Operand on the left is not equal to the operand on the right
<	Operand on the left is less than the operand on the right
>	Operand on the left is greater than the operand on the right
<=	Operand on the left is less than or equal to operand on the right

>=	Operand on the left is greater than or equal to the operand on the right

Here's an example using pseudo-code:

```
if (money > 600)
    print "I'm loaded"
else
    print "I'm not loaded"
```

and here's the C++ program that illustrates this example:

```
// test6_1.cpp

#include <iostream.h>
main()
{
    int money = 700;

    if (money > 600)
        cout << "I'm loaded \n";
    else
        cout << "I'm not loaded \n";
}
```

Compiling and running this program gives this output:

```
I'm loaded
```

This is because money is initialized to 700 at the start of the program. Here's a similar program that executes multiple statements:

```
// test6_2.cpp

#include <iostream.h>
main()
{
    int money = 700;

    if (money > 600)
        {
        cout  << "Pay gas bill";
        money = money - 40;
        cout << "Pay electric bill";

        money -= 65;
        cout << "Pay Visa account";
        money -= 145;
        if (money >= 600)
            cout << "I'm still loaded \n";
        else
```

```
            cout << "I'm not loaded anymore \n";
        }
    else
        cout << "I'm not loaded \n";
}
```

Compiling and running this program gives this output:

```
I'm not loaded anymore
```

This example illustrates the use of several features:

- We use the regular syntax to decrement money in this statement:

```
money = money - 40;
```

and the abbreviated syntax in this one:

```
money -= 65;
```

- We use braces to enclose the group of statements that follow the if condition:

```
if (money > 600)
    {
    cout  << "Pay gas bill";
    .
    .
        cout << "I'm not loaded anymore \n";
    }
```

- A second if-else control structure is enclosed within the first one:

```
if (money > 600)
    {
    .
    .
    if (money >= 600)
        cout << "I'm still loaded \n";
    else
        cout << "I'm not loaded anymore \n";
    }
    .
    .
```

If the second if-else control structure had multiple statements, those would have been enclosed within a second set of braces. You can enclose as many control structures as you wish, within each other! Just make sure that each structure has a logical beginning and ending.

6.3 THE WHILE STATEMENT

■ **The while statement is used to repeat the execution of a statement for as long as the condition it refers to is true.**

Here's the syntax:

```
while (this condition is true)
   {
   do this;
   and this;
   }
```

The conditions are once again expressed through relational operators. The same rules apply as the if statement. The parentheses are required around the condition being tested; multiple statements must be enclosed within braces; and each statement must be terminated with a semicolon.

We present a variant of the example presented in the previous section using the while statement instead of the if. First the pseudo-code:

```
if (money >= 700)
   {
   while (money > 200)
      {
      pay bill;
      reduce amount of money by amount of bill;
      }
   }
```

The best way to code this example would be through the use of an *array*, where each element in the array would represent the amount of the bill that is to be paid. However, since we haven't gotten to the chapter that explains arrays yet, we will set the amount of the bill to be paid to a constant, say $100. Here's the program:

```
// test6_3.cpp

#include <iostream.h>
main()
{
   int money = 700;

   if (money >= 600)
      {
      while (money > 200)
         {
         cout << "Pay bill";
         money -= 100;
         }
      cout << "Money left is: " << money << "\n";
```

```
    }
}
```

Here's the output:

```
Pay bill
Pay bill
Pay bill
Pay bill
Money left is 200
```

Notice

- The `while` statement is enclosed within the `if` statement.

- The statements inside the `while` statement are executed 4 times, until the condition that is being tested evaluates to false.

  100 is deducted from 700 four times, resulting in `money` being set to 200.   On the fifth iteration, the `while` condition evaluates to false, resulting in the ensuing `cout` statement being executed, which is part of the `if` loop.

  This brings us to a very important point.

- **If you code a `while` statement, don't forget to include some kind of condition that will result in a change in the condition that is being tested.**

  If you don't, the `while` loop will execute forever, because the condition that it will test will never change!!

6.4 THE DO-WHILE STATEMENT

- **The `do-while` statement is a variant of the `while` (although not as popular, most C++ programmers stick with the `while`).**

  Here's the syntax:

```
do
  {
  this;
  and this;
  }
  while (this condition is true)
```

The only difference between the while and the do-while statements is the place where the conditional test is performed. The while checks for the condition at the outset, while the do-while checks for the condition after having executed its conditions. This implies that

- **If the condition being tested is false at the outset, the** while **statements will never execute; on the other hand, the** do-while **statements will always execute atleast once.**

The example illustrates the use of the do-while loop:

```cpp
// test6_4.cpp

#include <iostream.h>
main()
{
    int money = 700;

    do
        {
        cout << "Pay bill";
        money -= 100;
        }
        while (money > 700)
    cout << "Money left is: " << money << "\n";
}
```

The output is:

```
Pay bill
Money left is 600
```

Notice

- At the start of the if loop, the amount of money available is 700.

- The do-while loop is executed, and 100 is subtracted from 700. money now has 600 stored in it.

- The while condition of the do-while fails.

Take a look at what happens if this program is rewritten using the while loop:

```cpp
// test6_5.cpp

#include <iostream.h>
main()
{
```

```
    int money = 700;

    while (money > 700)
        {
        cout << "Pay bill";
        money -= 100;
        }
    cout << "Money left is: " << money << "\n";
}
```

The output is

```
Money left is 700
```

The difference between these two loops should be clear to you now.

6.5 THE FOR STATEMENT

■ **The for loop contains an initialization, a test, and a reevaluation part.**

This is probably one of the most popular looping constructs. The syntax of the for statement looks like this:

```
for (initialize counter; perform conditional test; reevaluate
counter)
    {
    do this;
    and this;
    }
```

Here's a simple example, in simple English:

```
while money is greater than 200, pay the bills
```

Here it is in pseudo-code, using the for loop:

```
for (money=700; money>200; money -= 100)
    {
    pay bill;
    }
```

and here's the equivalent C++ program:

```
// test6_6.cpp

#include <iostream.h>
main()
{
```

```
for (money = 700; money > 200; money -= 100)
{
    cout << "Pay bill";
}
cout << "Money left is: " << money << "\n";
}
```

and the corresponding output:

```
Pay bill
Pay bill
Pay bill
Pay bill
Money left is 200
```

Compare it to the while loop, in test6_3.cpp:

```
// test6_3.cpp

#include <iostream.h>
main()
{
    int money = 700;

    if (money >= 600)
    {
        while (money > 200)
        {
            cout << "Pay bill";
            money -= 100;
        }
        cout << "Money left is: " << money << "\n";
    }
}
```

Now notice the following about test6_6.cpp:

■ The intialization is performed within the for statement itself:

```
for (money = 700; ......)
```

■ The conditional test is also performed within the for loop:

```
for (... ; money > 200; ...)
```

■ And so is the statement that would change the condition:

```
for (...; ...; money -= 100)
```

■ The first two parameters of the for statements are terminated by a semicolon. These two semicolons are required.

6.5.1 No Parameters in a for Loop

The interesting thing about a for statement is that each parameter can be
any valid C++ statement;

- **In a for statement, the first parameter need not be an
  initialization; the second need not be a test; and the third need
  not be a reevaluation; each of these can be any valid C++
  statements, including a null statement.**

  Following is perfectly valid:

  ```
  for (; a=2; b=3)
  {
      cout << "Hi \n";
  }
  ```

  The result of this for construct is that:

```
Hi
Hi
Hi


.

.
```

will be printed indefinitely.   This for construct represents no
initialization. The second parameter sets a to 2; which is a nonzero value.
The third parameter simply sets b to 3. Thus, the test condition always
evaluates to true, since the value of a is not changed in the third
parameter. Thus, the statements for this for loop will execute forever,
until you issue some kind of an interrupt to the operating system.
    You can even skip the second parameter, like this:

  ```
  for (;  ;  b=3)
  ```

  resulting in the same endless output.
  You can even skip all three, like this:

  ```
  for (; ; );
  ```

    Notice the terminating semicolon outside the parentheses, this is also
required, in addition to the two inside the parens. This statement will
result in your program hanging until you issue an interrupt; it is a do-
nothing forever loop.

6.5.2 Reevaluation Outside Parentheses

You can place the reevluation of the condition outside of the parentheses, like this:

```
// test6_8.cpp

#include <iostream.h>
main()
{
    for (money = 700; money > 200; )
    {
        cout << "Pay bill";
        money -= 100;
    }
    cout << "Money left is: " << money << "\n";
}
```

Notice the missing third parameter. The reevluation is performed, instead, in the body of the for loop.

6.6 THE SWITCH STATEMENT

■ **The switch statement is a construct which handles multiple if-else statements.**

Consider the following example:

```
if your are in your first year of college
    you are a freshman
else if you are in your second year
    you are a sophomore
else if you are in your third year
    you are a junior
else if you are in your fourth year
    you are a senior
else
    you're not in college
```

What you see is a list of options, only one of which should (theoretically) evaluate as true. The *swith-case-default* construct can be used to handle multiple alternative conditions such as these. Here's the syntax:

```
switch(on integer expression)
    {
    case constant 1:
        {
        do this;
```

```
        and this;
        }
    case constant 2:
        {
        do this;
        and this;
        }
    default:
        {
        do this;
        and this;
        }
```

- **The integer expression is any valid C++ expression that will yield an integer expression, which would evaluate to a true (nonzero) or false (zero) condition.**

case constant 1, case constant 2, and so on, represent labels. These are also constants.

- If the result of the integer expression matches one of the labels in the switch construct, then *the set of statement or statements* (more than two statements are enclosed within braces) for that label, *plus all subsequent case and default statements* are executed.

- **If there is no match, then that block of code is skipped.**

- **If no matches are found for the case labels, the default statements are executed.**

Returning to the example presented at the start of this section, assume that the number 1 represents a freshman, 2 a sophomore, 3 a junior, and 4 a senior. Here's the example in C++:

```cpp
// test6_7.cpp

#include <iostream.h>
main()
{
    int number_of_years = 3;

    switch(number_of_years)
    {
        case 1:
            cout << "I'm a freshman \n";
        case 2:
            cout << "I'm a sophomore \n";
        case 3:
            cout << "I'm a junior \n";
        case 4:
```

```
        cout << "I'm a senior \n";
    default:
        cout << "I'm not in college \n";
    }
}
```

The output of this program follows

```
I'm a junior
I'm a senior
I'm not in college
```

The switch is turned on for the value contained inside the parentheses, which is 3. The match is found on the case label which matches this constant (case 3). Then the statement for this case statement is executed, *plus all subsequent case statements as well!*

In most cases, we would like the program to execute only that block of statements which belong to the case statement on which a match is found. C++ allows us to do this through the use of the *break* statement. Thus, almost all switch case constructs coded contain a *break*.

■ **The** break **statement allows immediate exit from the control structure.**

We rewrite example test6_7.cpp with the break statement:

```
// test6_8.cpp

#include <iostream.h>
main()
{
    int number_of_years = 3;

    switch(number_of_years)
    {
      case 1:
        {
        cout << "I'm a freshman \n";
        break;
        }
      case 2:
        {
        cout << "I'm a sophomore \n";
        break;
        }
      case 3:
        {
        cout << "I'm a junior \n";
        break;
        }
      case 4:
```

```
      {
      cout << "I'm a senior \n";
      break;
      }
   default:
      cout << "I'm not in college \n";
   }
}
```

The output for this program is:

I'm a junior

Notice

- There is no break statement for the default case. Since this is the last case, we don't need a break here, control will pass out of the switch loop anyway.

- Braces are used to enclose the code of each case construct. This is because each case now contains more than one statement for it.

If there were no matches, then the statements following the default case would have executed.

6.6.1 The Order of Case Constructs

- The case constructs do not need to be in any specific order.

The thing to remember is that if you don't code the break statement, all cases below it will execute.

6.6.2 Switching On Characters

- **Character constants can be used instead of integers within the integer expression.**

These constants can be used to represent the labels as well. Remember that when the compiler evaluates a character constant, it breaks it down to its ASCII code, which is nothing more than an integer representation for that character.

Here's the same example using character constants:

```cpp
// test6_9.cpp

#include <iostream.h>
main()
{
    int school_year = 'J';

    switch(school_years)
    {
        case 'F':
            {
            cout << "I'm a freshman \n";
            break;
            }
        case 's':
            {
            cout << "I'm a sophomore \n";
            break;
            }
        case 'J':
            {
            cout << "I'm a junior \n";
            break;
            }
        case 'S':
            {
            cout << "I'm a senior \n";
            break;
            }
        default:
            cout << "I'm not in college \n";
    }
```

The output for this program is:

```
I'm a senior
```

Notice

- A small 's' is used to represent a sophomore

- A capital 'S' is used to represent a senior

- **Remember that only single constant values can be evaluated as labels.**
  Thus, only single characters can be used. We cannot switch on character strings.

6.6.3 Mixing Integers and Characters

■ **Integer and character constants can be freely intermixed within a switch construct.**

■ **Character constants will be broken down to their ASCII decimal equivalent.**

Here's an example that illustrates this feature:

```
// test6_10.cpp
#include <iostream.h>
main()
{
    char match = '1';

    switch(match)
    {
        case 1:
            {
            cout << "I'm in case 1 \n";
            break;
            }
        case 49:
            {
            cout << "I'm in case 49 \n";
            break;
            }
        case '2':
            {
            cout << "I'm in case 2 \n";
            break;
            }
        default:
            cout << "I'm in default \n";
    }
}
```

In this example, the variable match is set to the character constant 1. The switch is executed on this character constant. The output looks like this:

```
I'm in case 49
```

The reason for this is that 49 is the decimal ASCII equivalent of the character constant 1. Notice that no match is found for case 1; this is because 1 is a decimal number.

6.7 **THE** CONTINUE **AND** GOTO **STATEMENTS**

In the previous section we discussed the break statement. We add a discussion on the continue and goto statements statement, which are similar in functionality.

- **The break statement is used to break out of the existing loop and go straight to the test condition of the loop.**

    Here's a short example:

```
// test6_x.cpp
#include <iostream.h>
main()
{
    int i = 50;

    while (i <= 80)
    {
        i += 10;
        if (i == 80)
            continue;
        cout << "i is " << i << "\n";
    }
}
```

    The output for this program is:

```
i is 60
i is 80
```

    Notice that the statement

```
i is 70
```

is not output. The reason is this. When i is equal to 70, the continue statement is executed, resulting in control going directly to the test condition, without any subsequent statements in the loop being executed. Thus, the cout statement for i equal to 70 is never executed.

    We discuss the goto statement next.

- **The goto statement allows for unconditional jump from one place to another, wherever it is encountered.**

    Here's the previous example using a goto statement:

```
// test6_x.cpp
#include <iostream.h>
main()
```

```
{
   int i = 50;

   while (i <= 80)
   {
top_of_loop:   i += 10;
               if (i == 80)
                   goto top_of_loop;
               cout << "i is " << i << "\n";
   }
}
```

The output for this program is:

```
i is 60
i is 80
```

Notice the following statement:

```
top_of_loop:   i += 10;
```

top_of_loop is the name of a label. The goto statement directs execution to continue to whatever statement is prefixed with that label.

6.8 REVIEW

In this chapter, the following control structures were discussed:

- if and if-else statements

- the while statement

- the do-while statement

- the for statement

- the switch-case construct

All of these control structures represent different ways of implementing conditional logic inside a program.

Functions

7.1 INTRODUCTION

In this chapter, we will discuss how functions are put together in C++ programs.

- **A *function* is a self-contained block of code, the inner workings of which are invisible to the remainder of the program.**

Here's an analogy that will help you understand exactly what a function is.

7.2 AN ANALOGY

Assume you decide that you're getting really tired of the rat race and you need to take a week off in some exotic island in the Caribbean. Since you're far too busy to make the reservations yourself, you choose a travel agent to do all the work for you. The travel agent takes care of the air and hotel accommodations by calling the appropriate parties involved. Representatives of the airline issue the tickets and forward them to the travel agent. Representatives of the hotel issue the necessary vouchers, and also forward them to the travel agent. The travel agent mails the tickets and papers to your addresss, and you're all set!

You had a task to perform (get tickets and make hotel reservations), but you assigned these tasks to the travel agent. The travel agent contacted the appropriate personnel who issued the relevant tickets and vouchers. Exactly what the travel agent did to perform their duties is invisible to you. Exactly what the airline and hotel personnel did to issue the tickets and accommodations vouchers is invisible to the travel agent. All you know (and possibly care about) is the information you passed on to the travel agent (dates that you will travel, island that you wish to go to), what came back to you (the tickets and the vouchers), and the possible side effects (what this trip will cost you). Each of these people cooperated with the other to perform a function on their own. How each function was performed is invisible to the outside parties.

This is, in essence, what a C++ function is all about.

- **A function comprises a self-contained block of code that performs a specific task, and, if necessary, cooperates with other functions, to produce the final output.**

- **The inner workings of the function are invisible to the rest of the program.**

Values can be passed from one function to another, synonymous to the information that was being passed back and forth between yourself, the travel agent, and the hotel/air personnel. The concept of functions should now be clear to you.

All C++ programs comprise one function called main(). We'll discuss this next.

7.3 MAIN() AND FUNCTIONS

- **All C++ programs have a central entry point to the program called main().**

Within main(), there is no function, or any number of functions that can call other functions. Here are two examples that illustrate what has just been said.

```
//test7_1.cpp

#include <iostream.h>
main()
{
    cout << "This is main \n";
}
```

This program contains only one function, which is main(). Now take a look at test7_2.cpp. But first, here's the English version of what it's supposed to do.

```
Initialize a to 5
call a function called call_1
add 5 to the value stored in 5
come back to main
store the new value of a in another variable, called b
```

And here's the C++ version:

```
//test7_2.cpp

#include <iostream.h>
int call_1(int); // Notice function prototype

main()
{
    int a = 5;
    int b;

    b = call_1(a);

    cout << "a is " << a " b is " << b << "\n";
}
int call_1(a)
{
    a += 5;
    return a;
}
```

This program illustrates a number of important features about functions and how they are used in a C++ program. We will step through this program line by line and point out the significant features in each line.

The program starts by declaring the C++ class library iostream.h, this is necessary, if we are to use cout.

The next line is the declaration for a *function prototype*.

■ **A function prototype is used to indicate the name of the function that is expected to be called and defined later on in the body of the program.**

■ **A function prototype indicates not only the function's name, but also arguments and return type.**

The data type of value (if any) that will be sent to this function is called an *argument* (this is what you see in the parentheses). The data type of the value (if any) that will be returned by that function is called *return type* (this is what you see to the left of the function name). In our example, the function prototype states

```
int call_1(int);
```

that a function called `call_1()` will be defined, it will be sent one argument, which is of integer data type. This function will also return an integer data type.

The next four lines contain no suprises:

```
main()
{
    int a = 5;
    int b;
```

The next line requires a little bit more thought:

```
    b = call_1(a);
```

When the compiler reads this line, *it passes control from* `main()` *to the function referenced*. As it does so, *it passes the current value of a to* `call_1` *as well!* Let's continue with `call_1()`.

```
int call_1(a)
{
    a += 5;
    return a;
}
```

■ **The code that is used to specify what the function does (i.e., the body of the function) is called the *function definition*.**

Notice that the name, return type, and argument type of the function definition match the function prototype, which was encountered at the beginning of the program:

```
int call_1(int);     // function prototype

int call_1(a)        // function definition
```

The only difference is that the data type is replaced by the actual variable name that was sent in to it as a parameter. Also notice that

■ **The function prototype is terminated by a semicolon, while the name at the top of the function definition is not.**

Inside the function, 5 is added to the current value of a, and the statement

```
    return a;
```

is used to *return the value of* a *back to the calling function,* which happens to be main().

Back inside main(), the new value of a is stored in b, like this:

    b = call_1(a);

and cout is used to print the new values in both variables.

Now that you have a fair idea of how functions work, we will list some of the rules associated with functions and function calls.

7.4 FUNCTION PROTOTYPES MUST EXIST

- **All functions that are defined in a program must be declared as prototypes.**

Take a look at this program:

```
//test7_3.cpp
#include <iostream.h>

main()
{
    int a = 5;
    int b;

    b = call_1(a);
    cout << "a is " << a " b is " << b << "\n";
}
int call_1(a) // Notice that char is being returned
{
    a += 5;
    return a;
}
```

Compiling this program generates an error. This error is generated because the function prototype is missing.

7.5 PROTOTYPES MUST CORRESPOND TO DEFINITIONS

- **The name, argument or arguments, and return type of the prototypes must correspond to their function definition.**

We modify test7_1.cpp to illustrate what happens if this rule is not followed.

```
//test7_4.cpp
#include <iostream.h>
int call_1(int); // Notice function prototype

main()
{
    int a = 5;
    int b;

    b = call_1(a);
    cout << "a is " << a " b is " << b << "\n";
}
float call_1(a)  // Notice that char is being returned
{
    a += 5;
    return a;
}
```

Compiling this program also generates an error. This error is generated because the function prototype states that an integer is the return type, while the function definition states that it is float.

7.6 VOID ARGUMENT AND RETURN TYPES ARE VALID

- **The keyword void is used if there is no need to pass arguments to the function, or have the function return a value.**

Take a look at this program:

```
//test7_5.cpp
#include <iostream.h>
void call_1(void)    // Notice use of keyword void

main()
{
    cout << "This is main \n";
    call_1;
}
void call_1(void)
{
    cout << "This is call_1 \n";
}
```

Compiling this program gives us:

```
This is main
This is call_1
```

Notice the use of the keyword void for the return and argument types in the function definition. Also notice that this keyword is skipped when the function is actually called, and it reappears in the function definition.

7.7 RETURN STATEMENT MUST EXIST, IF VALUE IS RETURNED

- **As stated previously, the return type of the function in the function definition must correspond with its prototype.**

- **If a return type is not specified explicitly in the prototype, then a default return type of int is assumed by the compiler.**

However, please note that

- **Unless you insert a return statement in the function definition, the correct value will not be passed back to main().**

Remember that the inner workings of a function are transparent to the rest of the program. Unless a return statement is included in the function definition, the calling function will never know what happened there. (Values can be passed back and forth through arguments as well, but we will defer a discussion on that subject until we get to the chapter on pointers.)

7.8 FUNCTION NAMES NEED NOT BE UNIQUE

This one may catch you by surprise, but it's true.

- **Two or more distinct functions can actually have the same name. In C++, the term given to this feature is *function overloading*.**

This is a powerful capability of C++ that is not present in C, its counterpart language. Take a look at this program:

```
// test7_6.cpp

#include <iostream.h>

// notice two functions of same name
void sum(int i);
void sum(float j);
```

```
main(void)
{
    int i = 5;
    float j = 5.5;

    sum(i);      // call sum() to add integer
    sum(j);      // call sum() to add float
}

void sum(int i)
{
    i += 5;
    cout << "i is " << i << " \n";
}

void sum(float j)
{
    j += 5;
    cout << "j is " << j << " \n";
}
```

Compiling and running the program above will result in the following output:

```
i is 10
j is 10.5
```

What you see here is a very simple case of function overloading. The function name sum() is *overloaded*.

■ **In overloaded functions, the same function is given multiple definitions or implementations. The execution of the correct implementation is performed by the compiler, not the programmer.**

The compiler matches up the type of the arguments in the function call with the types in the function definition, and executes the one that matches the type of the argument in the function call. That's all there is to it.

Now let's modify the program and see what happens if different data types are sent to the two functions:

```
// test7_7.cpp

#include <iostream.h>
void sum(int i);
void sum(float j);

main(void)
{
```

```
    char i = 'c';
    float j = 3.14323;

    // send ASCII c to sum()
    // send floating point to sum()
    sum(i);
    sum(j);
}

void sum(int i)
{
    cout << "Inside sum(int) \n";
}

void sum(float j)
{
    cout << "Inside sum(float) \n";
}
```

This program compiles properly. The output is as follows:

```
Inside sum(int)
Inside sum(float)
```

Now how did the C++ compiler figure out which function to invoke each time? The process is really very simple. First, it compares the definition of overloaded functions with the definition parameters in the function call. If there is a match, then that function is implemented. If there is no match, then

- **The compiler performs type conversions and implements the function that allows the equivalent type conversion.**

In our example, sum(int) was called the first time around because the ASCII character 'c' was converted to integer, and thereby matched the function definition of sum(int).

The second time around, the value 3.14323 matched the data type of float, and sum(float) was called.

Now let's modify this program and see what happens if an integer is sent to a function that expects a character:

```
// test7_8.cpp

#include <iostream.h>

// sum(char) expects char as argument
// sum(float) expects float as argument
void sum(char);
void sum(float);
```

```
main(void)
{
    int i = 65;
    float j = 6.5;

    // send integer to sum()
    // send float to sum()
    sum(i);
    sum(j);
}

void sum(char i)
{
    cout << "Inside sum(char) \n";
}

void sum(float j)
{
    cout << "Inside sum(float) \n";
}
```

Compiling this program results in the following error message:

```
Error:   Ambiguity between 'sum(char)' and 'sum(float)'
```

This message was generated because the compiler expected to find a character sent to sum(char i) instead of an int, and it was unable to perform the necessary type conversions the other way. Function overloading will be discussed again in later chapters. For now, it is important that you understand the concept behind how it works in its simplest application. A summary follows:

- **In C++, more than one function can have the same name.**

- **The data types of the arguments in the function calls must match the data types in the function prototypes and definitions.**

- **If they don't, the compiler will perform type conversions. It will generate error messages if it is unable to match data types.**

7.9 MULTIPLE ARGUMENTS ARE VALID

- **Inside the calling function, the arguments that follow a function call are called *actual*.**

- **Inside the called functions, the arguments are called *formal*.**

All of our examples so far have been limited to passing one argument to the called function. However,

■ **You can send as many arguments as you wish to a function.**

The important thing is that the number and types of arguments in a function definition must always match their corresponding function prototype. If there is not exact correspondence, then the C++ compiler will attempt to convert the types of the actual arguments so that they can match the formal arguments in the called functions.

Here's an example in which multiple arguments are processed.

```
//test7_9.cpp
#include <iostream.h>

void call_1(int, int, int);
main()
{
    int a = b = c = 5;
    call_1(a, b, c);
}
void call_1(a, b, c)
{
    cout << "a is " << a << "\n";
    cout << "b is " << b << "\n";
    cout << "c is " << c << "\n";
}
```

Compiling this simple program gives this output:

```
a is 5
b is 5
c is 5
```

You should easily be able to understand the contents and output of this program.

7.9.1 The const Modifier

■ **You can precede an argument type with the modifier** const **to indicate that this argument cannot be changed.**

The argument to which it applies cannot be assigned a value or changed in any way.

The following program illustrates its use:

```
// test7_10.cpp
```

```
#include <iostream.h>

// const argument is sent as argument to function_1()
void function_1(const int i);

main(void)
{
    int i = 1;

    // i is passed as actual argument
    function_1(i);
}

// const modifier precedes argument name
void function_1(const int i)
{
    cout << " i is " << i << " \n";
}
```

Compiling and running this program give the following output:

```
i is 1
```

So far, so good. Now let's modify the program and change the value of i.

```
// test7_11.cpp

#include <iostream.h>
void function_1(const int i);

main(void)
{
    int i = 1;
    function_1(i);
}

void function_1(const int i)
{
    // const argument is incremented
    i++;
    cout << "i is " << i << " \n";
}
```

Compiling this program results in an error:

```
Error:   Cannot modify a const object
```

This is because an attempt is being made to change the value of the argument i, which was specified as type const.

7.9.2 The volatile **Modifier**

The volatile modifier is the flip side of const.

- The volatile keyword can be used to precede formal arguments to indicate that they are liable to be changed during the course of the normal execution of the program.

Declaring arguments as such also prevents the compiler from storing them in registers. Let's modify test7_11.cpp to use the keyword volatile instead of const:

```
// test7_12.cpp

#include <iostream.h>

// notice use of volatile keyword
void function_1(volatile int i);

main(void)
{
    int i = 1;
    function_1(i);
}

// notice use of keyword volatile
void function_1(volatile int i)
{
    i++;
    cout << "i is " << i << " \n";
}
```

This program gives the following output:

```
i is 2
```

7.9.3 DEFAULT INITIALIZERS CAN BE INCLUDED IN AN ARGUMENT LIST

- **In C++, you can have arguments default to values that you specify at the time that the function is called.**

Take a look at the following program:

```
// test7_13.cpp

#include <iostream.h>
void function_1(int i, int j);

main(void)
{
    int i = 1;
    int j;

    // j is initialized at time of function call
    function_1(i, j = 8);
}
void function_1(int i, int j)
{
    cout << "i is " << i << " \n";
    cout << "j is " << j << " \n";
}
```

Compiling this program results in the output:

```
i i 1
j is 8
```

This program illustrates two things in particular:

■ **The argument names can be declared in the function prototype, in addition to their data types.**

■ **Arguments can be initialized in the calling function.**

■ **Although arguments can be initialized at the time of the function call, please note that they cannot be initialized in the first line of the function definition.**

Take a look at this program:

```
// test7_14.cpp

#include <iostream.h>

void function_1(int i, int j);

main(void)
{
    int i=1;

    function_1(i);
}
```

```
// j is reinitialized in function definition
void function_1(int i, int j = 8)
{
    cout << "i is " << i << " \n";
    cout << "j is " << j << " \n";
}
```

Compiling this program gives an error:

```
Error:  Default argument value redeclared for parameter 'j'
```

Also, only the last or last set of arguments can be initialized. Take a look at this program:

```
// test7_15.cpp

#include <iostream.h>

// notice initialization of multiple arguments
void function_1(int i = 1, int j, int k = 2);

main(void)
{
    int i, k;
    int j = 2;

    function_1(i, j, k);
}

void function_1(int i, int j, int k)
{
    cout << "i is " << i << " \n";
    cout << "j is " << j << " \n";
    cout << "k is " << k << " \n";
}
```

Compiling this program results in the following error:

```
Error:  Default value missing following parameter 'i'
```

This program did not compile because C++ has another rule about default arguments. This rule states that

- **Only the last arguments in a parameter list can be initialized, the variable i is not one of the last.**

Okay. Let's modify test7_15.cpp to initialize the variables j and k only, and see what happens:

```
// test7_16.cpp

#include <iostream.h>

// only j and k are initialized
void function_1(int i, int j = 2, int k = 3);

main(void)
{
    int i = 1;
    int j, k;

    function_1(i);
}
void function_1(int i, int j, int k)
{
    cout << "i is " << i << " \n";
    cout << "j is " << j << " \n";
    cout << "k is " << k << " \n";
}
```

This program compiles properly. Here's the output:

```
i is 1
j is 2
k is 3
```

The output is as we expected.

Now we can summarize the rules that apply to default arguments in parameter lists.

- **Arguments can be initialized within function calls.**

- **Only the last arguments in the list can be assigned values.**

7.10 ELLIPSES CAN BE INCLUDED IN AN ARGUMENT LIST

- **In C++ you can enter ellipses in the formal paramater declaration of a function to indicate that the function will be called with different sets of arguments on different occasions.**

Type checking is not performed for these arguments. If you do not specify the correct argument data types in the format specification, then the results can be erratic, since there is no type checking.

Implementation of a variable number of arguments is a little bit complicated. The header file stdarg.h has to be included, and macros defined in this header file are used to obtain the necessary output. Since this is only a primer, and we haven't really described header files or macros yet. We will leave a detailed explanation of the implementation of these functions to your reference manual. For now, we just want you to be aware of this capability.

7.11 INLINE FUNCTIONS

When a function is called, there is a certain amount of overhead processing that goes along with it. In C++, you can reduce this overhead by preceding a function name at the time that it is defined with the keyword inline.

■ **The compiler compiles the code for the function defined as inline. Then, it simply substitutes this code for that function each time it is called within the program. This is called *inline expansion*.**

Since the function has already been compiled, the usual overhead incurred in a function call is avoided. Take a look at this program:

```
// test7_17.cpp

#include <iostream.h>
int increment(int i);

// notice keyword inline
inline increment(int i)
{
    i++;
    return i;
}

main(void)
{
    int i = 0;
    while (i < 3)
        {
        i = increment(i);
        cout << "i is " << i << " \n";
        }
}
```

The output for this program is:

```
i is 1
i is 2
i is 3
```

Okay. Now let's modify the program to move the definition of the inline function below main().

```
// test7_18.cpp

#include <iostream.h>
int increment(int i);

main(void)
{
    int i = 0;
    while (i <= 3)
        {
        i = increment(i);
        cout << "i is " << i << " \n";
        }
}

// inline function definition follows its function call
inline increment(int i)
{
    i++;
    return i;
}
```

Compiling this program gives an error. This is because

- **Inline functions must be defined before they are called.**

    Therefore, inline functions:

- Reduce function overhead

- Must be defined before they are called

7.12 RECURSIVE FUNCTIONS

- **In C++, a function can call itself. This is called a recursive function.**

    Take a look at this program:

```
// test7_19.cpp

#include <iostream.h>
void decrement(int i);

main(void)
{
    int i = 2;

    i = decrement(i);
```

```
    cout << "i is " << i << "\n";
}
int decrement(i)
{
    cout << "Inside decrement() \n";
    i--;
    if (i > 0)

        // function calls itself
        decrement(i);
    else
        return(i);
}
```

The output for this program looks like this:

```
Inside decrement()
Inside decrement()
i is 0
```

The function decrement() calls itself recursively until the test condition evaluates to *TRUE* (or a zero value). When i evaluates to zero, program control returns back to main().

7.13 REVIEW

In this chapter, we learned many interesting features about functions in C++:

■ main() returns a value of type int to the operating system.

■ Function prototypes are mandatory.

■ The return type, function name, and number and type of arguments in the prototype must agree with those in the actual function call and definition.

■ The compiler attempts to perform type conversions of arguments and return types whenever it can, to create a correspondence if one does not exist.

■ Function names can be *overloaded*, that is, assigned the same name. The decision of which function is executed at any time in the program is left up to the compiler, not the programmer.

- The const modifier notifies the compiler that a variable of this type cannot be modified.

- The volatile modifier notifies the compiler that a variable of this type can and probably will be modified.

- Default initializers can be assigned to function parameters in their prototypes.

- Functions can be called with variable number and types of parameters, via ellipses.

- C++ contains reference types. These are simply other names for the variables to which they are assigned.

- References provide a convenient way of passing arguments to functions by reference, rather than value.

- C++ allows the definition of inline functions, which helps reduce function call overhead.

- C++ allows recursive functions, that is, functions that can call themselves.

Arrays

8.1 INTRODUCTION

Often, data is grouped together into an ordered series. Consider, for example, the marks assigned to a class, the ages of all members of a family, or the names of the employees of an organization. Each of these examples groups data into a specific category (names, marks, ages), and assigns the same or different values to each member of that group. For example, the marks assigned to a class can be 85, 92, 97 and 88; the ages of the members of a family can be 35, 38 and 3 and 5 years old; the names of the employees of an organization can be Mary, John, and Sally. All of these examples can be represented as *arrays*.

- **An array is a collection of data; each data item is part of an ordered sequence.**

- **Each item of data is called an *element* of that array.**

This chapter will describe the characteristics of arrays, and how they are represented in a C++ program.

8.2 REPRESENTATION OF ARRAYS

Let's see how each element of the examples listed in the prior section are represented as arrays.

First, we have an array of the marks assigned to a class. The array can be called marks. There are four people in this class. Thus, this array will contain *four elements*. The data of this array is a collection of integers. Thus, this is an array of integers, or an integer array. This is how this array will be represented:

```
marks[0] = 85;
marks[1] = 92;
marks[2] = 95;
marks[3] = 88;
```

Notice that

- **Square brackets are used to specify the element of the array that is being processed.**

- **Counting starts are 0, not 1.**

The four statements above assign values to each element of the array. However, before an array can be assigned, it must be declared. (Remember, all variables must be declared before they can be used.) Here's the declaration of this array:

```
int marks[4];
```

Notice

- The number 4 is used to represent that there are four elements in this array. However, counting starts at the zero'th element, and stops at the third.

The reason for this will not be apparent to you until you get to the next chapter, which has to do with pointers. For now, we will give you a hint.

- **The last element of an array is always a terminating character, which is represented as '\0'. This terminating character is used to indicate the end of an array to the C++ compiler.**

This character is, in effect, invisible to you, but very significant to the compiler, and it is this element which is the fifth element of this array.

OK. Let's continue with the second example. Here we have an array of ages of the members of a family. This is how we could represent this array:

```
int age[4];          // This is the declaration

int age[0] = 35;     // Each element of array is assigned
int age[1] = 38;
int age[2] = 3;
int age[3] = 5;
```

Finally, we have an array of names of the employees of an organization. Here's how this array will be declared and assigned:

```
char names[3][6];    // This is the declaration

char names[0][6] = "Mary";
char names[1][6] = "John";
char names[2][6] = "Sally";
```

This array certainly looks a little different from the ones we defined before. Notice that

- **The name of the array is followed by two pairs of brackets.**

The array names is actually a *two-dimensional array* (as opposed to the one dimensional arrays we defined in the prior example. When this array is declared, the number within the first pair of square brackets defines the total number of elements that are contained in this array.

- The number within the second pair of brackets of a two-dimensional array indicates *the total number of elements contained within each element of that array.*

In our example, we have a two dimensional array that contains a total of 3 elements. Each element of the array is another array, of characters, the maximumu length assigned to each element is 6. Thus, each name within the array can not be longer than twelve characters.

Now we are in a position to summarize some of the features of arrays:

- **Arrays can be of any valid data type.**

- **Arrays can be single-dimensional, two-dimensional, and even more, such as three- or four-dimensional. Since arrays greater than two dimensions are rarely used, we will limit our discussion to up to two dimensions.**

- **Arrays must be declared before they can be used.**

- **Arrays can be assigned and initialized.**

8.3 How Arrays Are Stored in Memory

Before we continue with our discussion, let's take a moment to understand how arrays are stored inside a computer. It is important for you to understand this for several reasons. First, you need to know how arrays are stored in memory so that the concept of using a pointer to access the elements of an array is clear (this is a fundamental operation in most programs). Second, one of the common mistakes made by novice programmers is that they incorrectly estimate the size of an array. This results in the compiler either truncating significant values for it, or overwriting other variables in the program, since the compiler is unable to locate the last element of the array.

When an array is declared, the compiler reserves x number of adjacent locations in memory for it. When an element of an array is assigned, the compiler stores the appropriate value in that location. Going back to the first example:

```
int marks[4];
```

assume that the compiler reserves 4 spaces in memory, starting at the location designated by the number 5000. Given that it uses two bytes to store a data type of integer, the following spaces would be reserved:

Location in Memory	Contents
5000	85
5002	92
5004	95
5006	88

Notice that the location in memory is in increments of two for each element of the array. As noted previously, this is because the computer stores an integer number in two bytes of storage. If an array of double data types was declared, then it would be stored like this:

Location in Memory	Contents
5000	85
5004	92
5008	95

5012	88

The location in memory is now a multiple of four. This is because four bytes are required to store a double data type.

A character array would be stored like this:

Location in Memory	Contents
5000	'M'
5001	'a'
5002	'r'
5003	'y'
5004	'\0'

Notice that only one byte is used to store each character of the array. Remember that the declaration of the array called names[] looked like this:

```
char names[3][6];
```

The number 6 results in the compiler assigning 12 contiguous locations in memory for each element of this array. Thus, this array would be stored like this:

5000	5001	5002	5003	5004	5005
'M'	'a'	'r'	'y'	'\0'	
5006	5007	5008	5009	5010	5011
'J'	'o'	'h'	'n'	'\0'	
5012	5013	5014	5015	5016	5017
'S'	'a'	'l'	'l'	'y'	'\0'

Notice that memory location 5005 and 5011 are blank. This is because the first and second elements of name[] are only four characters long, and therefore occupy only five contiguous locations in memory. However, the compiler was instructed to reserve 6 bytes for it at the time that the array was declared. Also notice that each character string is terminated with the *null characater*, which is the '\0'.

8.4 OTHER FEATURES OF ARRAYS

In this section, other features related to arrays are illustrated via short C++ programs.

8.4.1 Initialization of Arrays at Declaration

■ **Arrays can be initialized at the time that they are declared.**

Take a look at this small program:

```
//test8_1.cpp
#include <iostream.h>

main()
{
    int marks[4] = {85, 92, 95, 88};

    cout << "Second element is: " << marks[1] << "\n";
}
```

The output for this program is:

```
Second element is 92
```

Notice

■ The array is iniatilized at the time that it is declared

■ Curly brackets are used to enclose the intitialization

■ The second element of the array is referenced as marks[1], since counting starts at the zero'th element

Here's another example:

```
//test8_2.cpp
#include <iostream.h>

main()
{
    int marks[3][2] = {{1,2},{3,4},{5,6}};

    cout << "Second element is: " << marks[1][1] << "\n";
}
```

The output for this program is:

4

If you work through the example, you should be able to understand the output.
Notice that

■ **A two-dimensional array is initialized at the time that it is declared.**

■ **Each element of the two-dimensional array is enclosed within its own pair of curly braces.**

■ **Each element is separated from the next by a comma.**

■ **The statement is terminated by a semicolon.**

8.4.2 Specification of Size Can Be Omitted

Arrays can also be declared like this:

```
//test8_3.cpp
#include <iostream.h>

main()
{
    int marks[] = {85, 92, 95, 88};

    cout << "Second element is: " << marks[1] << "\n";
}
```

The output for this program is:

Second element is 92

Notice

■ The size of the array is not specified

This declaration works only because the array is initialized right away. The compiler checks the number of elements that it is initialized to, and assigns storage space for an array of that size. If marks[] had been initialized to 8 numbers, than the compiler would have assumed that marks[] is an array comprised of 9 elements.

8.4.3 Arrays Can Be Passed to Functions

■ **Arrays can be sent back and forth between functions.**

Recall that when a variable is sent to a function, a copy of its value is sent, instead of the actual variable. Please note that this rule does not apply to arrays.

■ **When arrays are sent to functions, their actual values are manipulated.**

Here's an example:

```
//test8_5.cpp
#include <iostream.h>

main()
{
    void modify(int);        // function prototype
    int marks[] = {85, 92, 95, 88};

    modify(marks);

    cout << "Second element is: " << marks[1] << "\n";
}
void modify(marks[])
{
    marks[1] -= 10;
    return;
}
```

The output for this program is:

```
Second element is 82
```

Notice

■ The array marks[] is defined inside of main(). It is not redefined inside the function called modify().

There is no need to redefine it in the called function, since storage has already been allocated to this array at the time that it was declared in main(). Please note that there is an exception to this rule, which applies to two-dimensional arrays. If a two-dimensional array is passed to a function, its second subscript (i.e., the size of each element of the array) must be passed as well.

■ When modify() is called within main(), the size of the array that is sent to it as an argument is not specified, only the name. The square brackets are skipped as well.

■ **In C++, the zero'th element of an array can be referenced simply by its name.**

For example, the following statement

```
marks = 90;
```

will result in the zero'th element of the array being assigned. Subsequent elements of the array can be accessed simply by adding the appropriate element number to the name. For example

```
marks + 1 = 92
```

will result in marks[1] being modified.

■ In the function definition, the size of marks[] is once again skipped.

■ 10 is subtracted from the second element of marks[].

■ The correct value of marks[] is output in main(), although its value was modified in modify().

This is because the actual contents of the array are sent to the called function, instead of a copy of these values.

8.5 REVIEW

This chapter described arrays and how they are represented and stored inside a computer. We learned how to initialize arrays at the time that they are declared, and how they can be manipulated inside functions.

Pointers

9.1 INTRODUCTION

Pointers are one of the most powerful features of C++. They are also high on the list of those items that beginners find most difficult to understand. In this chapter, we will explain pointers in great detail. In subsequent chapters, you will learn how they are essential to the implementation of some of the most powerful features of C++; these are *classes*, *derived classes*, *virtual functions*, and *abstract classes*.

9.2 AN ANALOGY

The best way to explain the concept of pointers is with an analogy. Assume you are friends with the Clinton family. The Clintons are friends with the Kennedys. You would like to know how many people live at the Kennedy residence. You don't know where they live, but the Clintons do.

Assume that the Clintons live at house number 8364. This is how you would go about obtaining the information you need:

1. Go to house number 8364.
2. Obtain the Kennedy's house number.
3. This is house number 9381.
4. Go to house number 9381.
5. Find out how many people live there.

If we could narrow down this chain of events to just names and numbers, we would rewrite like this:

Address	Name	Information Received
8364	Clinton	9381
9381	Kennedy	5

Note that it was necessary for you to find the Kennedy address through the Clinton family. The Clintons, so to speak, pointed the way to the Kennedys.

Now let's bring C++ into the picture. Assume that clinton and kennedy are defined as integer variables in a program. In our example, clinton is a *pointer* to kennedy.

■ **A pointer is a variable that contains the address of another variable and, in this "indirect" way, points to that variable.**

Here's another look at these relationships:

clinton (name)	9381 (contents)	kennedy (name)	5 (contents)
	8364 (address)	9381 (address)	

At address 8364, we obtained the number 9381. At address 9381, we obtained the number 5. We can represent this information in columnar format like this:

Name	Address	Contents
clinton	8364	9381
kennedy	9381	5

So what is the number 9381? It is the value stored at the address 8364, or the *contents of the address* 8364. 9381 is also the address of the variable kennedy. And what is the number 5? It is the value stored at address 9381. 9381, as stated previously, is the address of the variable kennedy. Thus, the number 5 is the *contents of what is stored at the address* of the variable kennedy.

Let's substitute words for numbers in the contents column:

Name	Address	Contents
clinton	8364	Address of kennedy
kennedy	9381	Contents of what is stored at the address kennedy

If the words *address of* could be represented by the symbol & and *contents of* could be represented by *, we could rewrite these relationships like this:

Name	Address	Contents
clinton	8364	&kennedy
kennedy	9381	*(&kennedy)

We can go one step further and assign the corresponding values to the names:

```
clinton = &kennedy; // line 1
kennedy = *(&kennedy); // line 2
```

Substituting the assignment of clinton in line 2:

```
kennedy = *(clinton);  // rewrite line 2
```

As stated before, clinton is a pointer to kennedy. This is a unique data type. Thus, it has a unique declaration as well. Pointers are declared like this:

```
int *clinton;    // pointer type is declared
```

The above statement defines a pointer called clinton. This pointer will point to an integer data type.

And now, a short program that illustrates these relationships:

```
//test9_1.cpp
#include <iostream.h>

main()
{
    int *clinton;     // clinton is a pointer to an integer
    int kennedy;      // kennedy is not a pointer
```

```
    kennedy = 5;   // 5 is stored in kennedy
    clinton = &kennedy; // clinton is made to point to kennedy
    cout << "The value stored at kennedy is " << kennedy << "\n";
    cout << "The value stored at kennedy is " << *(&kennedy) <<
"\n";
    cout << "The value stored at kennedy is " << *carter << "\n";
}
```

The output for this program is:

```
The value stored at kennedy is 5
The value stored at kennedy is 5
The value stored at kennedy is 5
```

This program illustrates several features:

- **When a variable is referenced by its name, its contents are being referenced.**

This is illustrated by the first cout statement, which prints kennedy. The contents of kennedy are output.

- **The contents of a variable can also be output by *dereferencing* it.**

Dereferencing is illustrated by the second cout statement.

- **The contents of a variable can be printed indirectly, i.e., by *dereferencing the pointer that was made to point to it*.**

This is illustrated by the third cout statement.

And now, some very important points to remember:

- **A pointer to a data type must first be declared, just like any other data type.**

- **This pointer must then be made to point to something of that data type.**

If you do not adhere to these two rules, then your pointers will contain garbage in them.

Going back to the sample program, clinton is defined as a pointer to an integer data type. Then, it is made to point to the address of kennedy. The address of kennedy is obtained by prefixing the address of operator (&) to its name. The contents of what is stored at the kennedy address is obtained via the indirection operator, the asterisk:

```
*(&kennedy) or *carter
```

And that's all that pointers are. *It is essential that you understand the entire contents of what you have read in this chapter so far, before continuing.* Please take a moment now to review the previous pages.

9.3 ADDRESSES IN MEMORY

■ **When a variable is declared, it is assigned storage some place in the memory of the computer.**

Take another look at the program that was presented in the previous section:

```
//test9_1.cpp
#include <iostream.h>

main()
{
    int *clinton;    // clinton is a pointer to an integer
    int kennedy;     // kennedy is not a pointer

    kennedy = 5;  // 5 is stored in kennedy
    clinton = &kennedy; // clinton is made to point to kennedy

    cout << "The value at kennedy is " << kennedy << "\n";
    cout << "The value at kennedy is " << *(&kennedy) << "\n";
    cout << "The value at kennedy is " << *clinton << "\n";
}
```

Notice that a pointer is declared (clinton) and an integer variable is declared. Based on what has just been said, it follows that both clinton and kennedy are assigned storage some place in the computer.

We also mentioned that the address of operator (&) is used to obtain the address of a variable. Let's add some code to test9_1.cpp, to see what this address is:

```
//test9_2.cpp
#include <iostream.h>

main()
{
    int *clinton;    // clinton is a pointer to an integer
    int kennedy;     // kennedy is not a pointer

    kennedy = 5;  // 5 is stored in kennedy
    clinton = &kennedy; // clinton is made to point to kennedy
```

```
    cout << "The value at kennedy is " << kennedy << "\n";
    cout << "The value at kennedy is " << *(&kennedy) << "\n";
    cout << "The value at kennedy is " << *clinton << "\n";

    cout << "&kennedy is " << &kennedy << "\n";
    cout << "clinton is " << clinton << "\n";
}
```

The output for this program looks like this:

```
The value stored at kennedy is 5
The value stored at kennedy is 5
The value stored at kennedy is 5
&kennedy is 0x1b02
clinton is 0x1b02
```

The following diagram will help you visualize exactly what is going on:

Variable Name	Stored at this location in memory	Contains
kennedy	0x1b02	5
clinton		0x1b02

The number 0x1b02 is a location in memory expressed in hexadecimal. kennedy and clinton are both stored in different locations in memory. The contents of what is stored at these memory locations are indicated by what you see in the third column. As you can see, the contents of what is stored in kennedy is 5; and the contents of what is stored in clinton is *nothing more than the location in memory of where kennedy is stored.* These locations are represented by numbers.

And now a synopsis of pointers and pointer notation:

- **Pointers must be declared, just like any other data type. The data type name, such as int, char, double, etc., must precede the pointer name in the declaration.**

- **The indirection operator (*) must precede the pointer name in the declaration.**

- **Pointers must be made to point to something, or they will contain garbage.**

- **The address of operator (&) must precede the name of the variable that pointers are made to point to.**

■ **Pointers can exist for any valid data type.**

9.4 POINTERS TO ARRAYS

In Chapter 8, we described how arrays are stored in adjacent locations in memory. Here's a short program that outputs the memory locations that an array is stored in:

```
//test9_3.cpp
#include <iostream.h>

main()
{
   int i;
   int array[4] = {10, 20, 30, 40};

   for (i=0; i<4; i++)
   {
      cout << "array[" << i << "] is " << array[i] << "\n";
      cout << "and it is stored at " << &array[i] << "\n";
   }
}
```

The output for this program is:

```
array[0] is 10
and it is stored at 0x1ae0
array[1] is 20
and it is stored at 0x1ae2
array[2] is 30
and it is stored at 0x1ae4
array[3] is 40
and it is stored at 0x1ae6
```

As you can see, each variable is stored in two bytes of memory. Notice the notation that is used to output the location in memory of each element of the array. It is the same as we would have used to obtain the location in memory of integer, character, or any other valid data types. Along the same lines,

■ **The contents of what is stored at the address of each element of the array can be acquired through the use of the indirection operator.**

Here's the modified program that illustrates this:

```
//test9_4.cpp
#include <iostream.h>
```

```
main()
{
    int array[4] = {10, 20, 30, 40};

    for (i=0; i<4; i++)
    {
        cout << "array[" << i << "] is " << array[i] << "\n";
        cout << "and it is stored at " << &array[i] << "\n";
        cout << "using the indirection operator, it is "
            << *(&array[i]) << "\n";
    }
}
```

The output is:

```
array[0] is 10
and it is stored at 0x1aee
using the indirection operator, it is 10
array[1] is 20
and it is stored at ox1af0
using the indirection operator, it is 20
array[2] is 30
and it is stored at 0x1af2
using the indirection operator, it is 30
array[3] is 40
and it is stored at ox1af4
using the indirection operator, it is 40
```

Notice that the contents of each element of the array are output using the regular notation (array[0]) and they are also output using the indirection operator (*(&array[0]).

In the previous chapter, we also mentioned that the name of an array is equivalent to its zero'th element. As a matter of fact,

- **Each element of the array can be referenced simply by adding the correct number of offsets to the name.**

Here's an example:

```
//test9_5.cpp
#include <iostream.h>
main()
{
    int array[4] = {10, 20, 30, 40};

    cout "array is " << array << "\n";
    cout "array + 1 is" << array + 1 << "\n";
    cout "array + 2 is" << array + 2 << "\n";
    cout "array + 3 is" << array + 3 << "\n";
}
```

The output for this program is:

```
array is 0x1af4
array + 1 is 0x1af6
array + 2 is 0x1af8
array + 3 is 0x1afa
```

Notice that the address of each element of the array is output. The contents of what is stored at these addresses can be obtained by using the indirection operator, like this:

```
//test9_6.cpp
#include <iostream.h>

main()
{
        int array[4] = {10, 20, 30, 40};

        cout "array is " << array << "\n";
        cout "and its contents are " << *(array) << "\n";
        cout "array + 1 is" << array + 1 << "\n";
        cout "and its contents are " << *(array + 1) << "\n";
        cout "array + 2 is" << array + 2 << "\n";
        cout "and its contents are " << *(array + 2) << "\n";
        cout "array + 3 is" << array + 3 << "\n";
        cout "and its contents are " << *(array + 3) << "\n";

}
```

and here's the output:

```
array is 0x1b20
and its contents are 10
array + 1 is 0x1b22
and its contents are 20
array + 2 is 0x1b24
and its contents are 30
array + 3 is 0x1b26
and its contents are 40
```

Summarizing

■ **The address of the element of an array can be acquired in either of the following ways:**

```
&array[i]
```

or

```
array + i
```

■ **The contents of what is stored in each element of an array can be acquired in either of the following ways:**

```
array[i]
```

or

```
*(array + i)
```

OK. Now there's another way that the contents and memory locations of each element of an array can be output. And this is through a pointer to this array. Here's how:

```
//test9_7.cpp
#include <iostream.h>

main()
{
    int *ptr, i;
    int array[4] = {10, 20, 30, 40};

    ptr = array;

    for (i=0; i<4; i++)
    {
        cout << "array[" << i << "] is " << *ptr << "\n";
        cout << "and it is stored in memory location "
             << array + i << "\n";
        ptr++;
    }
}
```

The output for this program looks like this:

```
array[0] is 10
and it is stored in memory location 0x1ae6
array[1] is 20
and it is stored in memory location 0x1ae8
array[2] is 30
and it is stored in memory location 0x1aea
array[3] is 40
and it is stored in memory location ox1aec
```

Notice

■ ptr is declared as a pointer to an integer. This makes sense, since it will be made to point to an *array of integers*.

- ptr is made to point to the zero'th element of the array by assigning it to the name of the array.

- **The zero'th element of an array is also called its *base address*.**

- Each element of the array is output simply by incrementing ptr and printing the contents of what is stored in the locations in memory that are being pointed to by ptr.

9.5 POINTERS TO STRINGS

- **A string is nothing more than an array of ASCII characters.**

A string of characters is represented like this:

```
char name[5] = "Mary";
```

where char[0], (the base address of the array), contains the letter M. The location char[1] contains the letter a, char[2] contains the letter r, and char[3] contains the letter y. char[4] will contain the terminating null character, which is \0. These charactes are stored in contiguous locations in memory. The contents of this array can be manipulated via a pointer to this array. The next program demonstrates how:

```
//test9_8.cpp
#include <iostream.h>

main()
{
char name[5] = "Mary";
char *ptr_char;     // this is pointer to char

//ptr_char is set to the base address of the character array
ptr_char = name;
*(ptr_char+0) = 'G';

cout << "name is " << name;
}
```

The output for this program is:

```
name is Gary
```

As you can see, ptr_char is made to point to the base address of the array. The contents of what is stored at the base address of this array is modified via the statement:

```
*(ptr_char+0) = 'G';
```

This statement could also have been represented like this:

```
*(ptr_char) = 'G';
```

Notice that G is enclosed in single quotes. This is because we are modifying only one character of this array. Enclosing it in double quotes would result in G being represented as a string, i.e., it would be terminated by a null character, and occupy two bytes in memory.

Here's the same concept again:

```
//test9_9.cpp
#include <iostream.h>

main()
{
char name[4] = "Mary";
char *ptr_char;      // this is pointer to char

//ptr_char is set to the base address of the character array
ptr_char = name;
*(ptr_char+2) = 'n';

cout << "name is " << name;
}
```

The output for this program looks like this:

```
name is Many
```

Summarizing,

■ **A string is an array of characters.**

■ **Strings can be accessed and manipulated via pointers to characters.**

■ **The base address of a string variable can be obtained via its name.**

■ **Each subsequent element of the array can be obtained by adding the appropriate offset to name.**

■ **The base address of a string constant can be obtained by reference to that string.**

9.6 POINTERS AS ARGUMENTS IN FUNCTIONS

In the chapter on functions, we mentioned that arguments that are variables can be sent to functions. However, only a copy of these arguments are sent to the function. If this variable is manipulated inside the function, then the value of the actual variable remains unaltered. *However,*

■ **If a pointer to a variable is sent as an argument, the actual contents of that variable can be modified.**

Here's a simple example that illustrates how:

```
//test9_10.cpp
#include <iostream.h>

char name[4] = "Mary";
char *ptr;
void modify(char *ptr);    // function prototype

main()
{
    ptr = name;        // set ptr to base address of name[];
    modify(ptr);
    cout << "name is " << name << "\n";
}

void modify(char *ptr)
{
    *(ptr + 2) = 'n';
}
```

The output for this program is:

```
name is Many
```

First, ptr is set to point to the base address of the array name[]. Then, modify() is called, and this pointer is passed as an argument to the function modify(). Inside this function, the third element of the array that this pointer is pointing to is modified. The new contents of name() are output back in main().

Summarizing,

- **One function can not directly change the contents of a variable. However, these contents can be changed indirectly, via a pointer to that variable.**

9.7 OPERATIONS PERMITTED ON POINTERS

- **Pointers can be incremented, decremented, compared.**

- **Values can be added and subtracted from pointers.**

- **If two pointers point to objects of the same type, then they can be subtracted from each other.**

This assumes, of course, that you are executing a logically correct operation.

The following operations on pointers are not permitted:

- **Multiplication of a pointer by a constant**

- **Division of a pointer by a constant**

- **Multiplication of two pointers**

- **Division of one pointer into another**

- **Subtraction of a pointer from a constant**

- **Addition of two pointers**

Table 9.1 summarizes the operations that are and are not permitted on pointers, and the results obtained from executing them. Here's the example that Table 9.1 builds on:

```
//test9_11.cpp
#include <iostream.h>

main()
{
    int *ptr1, *ptr2;
    int a[2], b;

    // ptr1 points to first element of integer array a[]
    // ptr2 points to second element of integer array a[]

    ptr1 = &(a[0]);
```

```
ptr2 = &(a[1]);

// Assume that a[0] is stored in memory location 1000.
// Our computer used two bytes to store an integer.
// Therefore, a[1] will be stored in memory location 1002.

    .
    .
    .
}
```

The last column of table 9.1 indicates the result of the exeuction of the expression in the **Representation** column. All results are based on the initial values of the pointers, i.e., ptr1 contains 1000, and ptr2 contains 1002.

Table 9.2 Results of Operations on Pointers

Operation	Permitted	Representation	Result
Increment pointer	Yes	ptr1++;++ptr1; ptr2++;++ptr2;	ptr1 = 1002 ptr2 = 1004
Decrement pointer	Yes	ptr1--;--ptr1; ptr2--;--ptr2;	ptr1 = 998 ptr2 = 1000

Compare pointers	Yes	if (ptr1 > ptr2)
		for (;ptr1 <
		ptr2;ptr1++;)
		while (ptr1 < ptr2)
			False
			Will loop
			once
			True

Add integer to pointer	Yes	ptr1 += 5; ptr2 += 5;	ptr1 = 1005 ptr2 = 1007
Subtract integer from pointer	Yes	ptr1 -= 5; ptr2 -= 5;	ptr1 = 995 ptr2 = 997
Subtract 1 pointer from another	Yes	b = ptr2 - ptr1	b = 2
Subtract a pointer from a constant	No	b = 8 - ptr1; b = 10 - ptr2	Won't compile
Add two pointers	No	b = ptr1 + ptr2;	Won't compile
Multiply a pointer by a constant	No	b = ptr1 * 5;	Won't compile

Dividie a pointer by a constant	No	b = ptr1 / 5;	Won't compile
Multiply two pointers	No	b = ptr1 * ptr2;	Won't compile
Divide one pointer by another	No	b = ptr1 / ptr2;	Won't compile

9.8 REFERENCE ARGUMENTS

In this section a `reference` will be described. References can be sent to functions, instead of pointers, and you will see how in just a little bit.

- **A *reference* is simply another name for a variable.**

Take a look at the following code:

```
// test9_12.cpp

#include <iostream.h>
main(void)
{
    // devil is assigned a value
    // satan is another name for devil
    int devil = 666;
    int &satan = devil;

    cout << "devil is " << devil << " \n";
    cout << "satan is " << satan << " \n";
}
```

The program's output is:

```
devil is 666
satan is 666
```

The variable devil, which is of type integer, is initialized to 666. Then, the reference type satan is set equal to devil. A reference is implied when the & sign is used to precede its name. A reference must be initialized at the time that it is declared. Restating a little bit differently, satan is simply another name for devil. devil was initialized to 666. After setting the reference type satan equal to devil, satan also contains the value 666. Notice that the value of satan is output, and not &satan. &satan would give the address of where this reference type is stored in memory.

Let's change the value of the reference, and see what happens:

```cpp
// test9_13.cpp

#include <iostream.h>
main(void)
{
    int devil = 666;
    int &satan = devil;

    cout << "devil is " << devil << " \n";
    cout << "satan is " << satan << " \n";

    // value of satan is changed
    satan = 999;
    cout << "devil is " << devil << " \n";
    cout << "satan is " << satan << " \n";
}
```

The output for this program follows:

```
devil is 666
satan is 666
devil is 999
satan is 999
```

As you can see, changing the value of the reference type satan results in changing the value of the variable to which it was assigned, i.e., devil. This makes sense. After all, satan is just another name for devil!

Now that you understand what a reference is, let's see how it can be used as an argument in functions.

Recall that arguments are passed to functions by value. In other words, the variable itself is not passed to the function, only a copy of that variable. What this meant for you as a programmer was that if you wanted to change the value of that variable in the called function, you had to pass a pointer to it, and then manipulate its contents via that pointer. However,

■ **In C++, you can pass arguments by value and by reference.**

Take a look at the program below which uses a reference instead of a pointer to change the contents of i in the called function.

```cpp
// tests9_14.cpp

#include <iostream.h>
int function_1(int j);
```

```
main(void)
{
    int i = 66;

    // j is a reference to integer type
    int &j = i;

    cout << "j is " << j << " i is " << i << " \n";

    // send reference to i
    i = function_1(j);

    cout << "j is " << j << " i is " << i << " \n";
}

int function_1(j)
{
    j = 3;
    return j;
}
```

Compiling and running this program will result in the following output:

```
j is 66 i is 66
j is 3 i is 3
```

The argument j is passed by reference, not value. Therefore, this argument provides direct access to the object that it was made to reference (i.e., i), and its contents are modified without the use of pointers in the called function.

Let's review references:

- References are just other names for the variables to which they are assigned. A reference is prefixed with an & sign on the left side of the assignment operator, and must be initialized at the time that it is defined.

- References provide a convenient way of passing arguments to functions by reference, instead of value, as was the case in C.

9.9 REVIEW

This chapter described pointers and references. A pointer contains the location in memory of a variable. It must be declared and then initialized to point to something.

We learned how to declare and use pointers to different data types, such as arrays and strings. We also learned how pointers can be used to change the actual values of variables inside functions. Operations that can and cannot be performed on pointers were listed. The chapter concluded with a discussion on references, and how they can be used to modify variables inside function calls, instead of pointers.

Structures

10.1 INTRODUCTION

In *Webster's Encyclopedic Unabridged Dictionary*, a structure is defined as:

"...mode of building, construction, or organization; arrangement of parts, elements, or constituents..."

"...anything composed of parts arranged together in some way; an organization..."

The keyword `structure` in C++ is used to convey the same concept in the English language. Let's see how.

10.2 A STRUCTURE, THE CONCEPT

Real world data can often be grouped together in a specific manner. For example, a family can be defined as containing a husband, a wife, and one or more children. A class of students can be defined by its name, and the number of boys and girls in it. Employees in a company can be grouped together by their names, their title, and their salaries.

■ **C++ allows us to define collections of groups of data in the form of a structure.**

- **A structure is a compound data type. It gathers together, in a fixed pattern, different pieces of information, and provides a name.**

Examples will help you understand the concept just described.

10.3 STRUCTURES, DECLARATION

As indicated in the previous section, a family can be defined as containing a husband, a wife, and one or more children. This is how the data could be recorded:

Table 10.1 A Family Structure

Husband	Wife	Children (Number)
John	Kathy	2
Kenneth	Sylvia	3
Peter	Joyce	1

This information would be translated into a C++ structure like this:

```
structure family
    {
    char husband[10];
    char wife[10];
    int children;
    };
```

This is a structure declaration.

- **The keyword** structure **(you can shorten this to** struct**) indicates to the compiler that a structure data type is being declared.**

The *name* or *tag* of this structure is family.

- **The contents of the structure are called** *members*.

The members of the structure family are husband, wife and children. husband and wife are character data types, and children is an integer data type. The following rules apply to the syntax:

- **The structure declaration must start with the keyword structure or struct.**

■ This keyword must be followed by the structure name or tag.

■ An opening curly brace follows the structure name. The structure members and their data types are enclosed within this opening brace and its corresponding curly brace. Each member data type is terminated by a semicolon.

■ The closing brace is followed by a semicolon.

Please note that

■ A structure declaration only defines the template or the form of the structure. The compiler does not reserve space in memory at the time that it encounters a structure declaration.

So when does a compiler assign memory to a structure? The answer is *when variables of that structure type are declared.* This is how structures which are of the structure type family are declared:

```
struct family Gerard, Cole, Chen;
```

Thus, Gerard, Cole, and Chen are defined as structures of type family. The compiler will now assign memory to these structures. Assume that assignment starts at memory location 1001. Storage would be assigned like this:

Name	Husband	Wife	Children
Gerard	1001 - 1010	1011 - 1020	1021 - 1022
Cole	1023 - 1032	1033 - 1042	1043 - 1044
Chen	1045 - 1054	1055 - 1064	1065 - 1066

As you can see, ten bytes each are assigned to husband and wife members. Two bytes of storage are assigned to children member, since it is defined as an integer, and an integer is stored in two bytes on our computer.

Please also note that

■ Structure members will always be assigned space in the order in which they are declared.

OK. Let's take a look at the structure declarations of the other two examples presented.

Table 10.2 A Class Structure

Class Name	Number of Boys	Number of Girls
Math	10	15
Computer Science	13	10
Economics	7	9

This information would be translated into a C++ structure like this:

```
structure class
    {
    char class_name[];
    int number_of_boys;
    int number_of_girsl;
    };
```

and variables of this type of structure would be declared like this:

```
struct class Math, Computer_Science, Economics;
```

Table 10.3 An Employee Structure

Employee Name	Title	Salary
Berkowitz	Senior Analyst	85000
Carlston	Manager	87000
Reis	Programmer	60000

This information would be translated into a C++ structure like this:

```
structure employee
    {
    char name[];
    char title[];
    int salary;
    };
```

Structures of type employee would be declared like this:

```
struct employee Berkowitz, Carlston, Reis;
```

10.4 ASSIGNMENT OF STRUCTURE MEMBERS

■ **Structure members can be assigned values via the assignment operator.**

Thereafter, each member can be referenced as follows:

structure_name.member_name

The following example will help you understand what has just been said:

```
//test10_1.cpp
#include <iostream.h>

main()
{
struct family
   {
   char husband[10];
   char wife[10];
   int children;
   };

struct family Gerard = {"John","Kathy",2};
struct family Cole = {"Kenneth","Sylvia",3};
struct family Chen = {"Peter","Joyce",1};

Gerard.children = 0;
Cole.children = 2
Chen.children = 4;

cout << "Gerard children: " << Gerard.children << "\n";
cout << "Cole children: " << Cole.children << "\n";
cout << "Chen.children << Chen.children "\n";

}
```

The output for this program is

```
Gerard children: 0
Cole children: 2
Chen children: 4
```

Summarizing:

■ **Structure members are referenced by prefixing member name with the structure name (*not* the template name) that they belong to.**

- **Structure members can be assigned values through the assignment operator.**

Structure members can be assigned values like this as well:

```
struct family
    {
    char husband[10];
    char wife[10];
    int children;
    } Gerard = {"John","Kathy",2},
        Cole = {"Kenneth","Sylvia",3},
        Chen = {"Peter","Joyce",1};
```

Notice that

- **Each structure name is separated from the next by a comma.**

- **The statement is terminated by a semicolon.**

10.5 ARRAYS OF STRUCTURES

- **Arrays of structures can be declared using the same syntax as arrays of other data types.**

Take a look at the following program:

```
//test10_x.cpp
#include <iostream.h>

main()
{
    struct employee
    {
    char employee_num;
    int salary;
    };

    struct employee a[3];  // a[] is an array of structures

    a[0].employee_num = 9901;
    a[0].salary = 85000;

    a[1].employee_num = 1026;
    a[1].salary = 66000;

    a[2].employee_num = 3908;
```

```
    a[2].salary = 55000;

    cout << "Employee Number  Salary\n "
    for (i=0; i<=2; i++)
    {
        cout << a[i].employee_num << " "
            << a[i].salary << "\n";
    }
}
```

The output for this program is:

```
Employee Number  Salary
9901 85000
1026 66000
3908 5000
```

Notice that salary is declared as double. This was necessary, in order to accommodate the high salaries of its employees.

Thus,

■ **The syntax for referencing members of arrays of structures is:**

array_name[index].member_name

Storage for this array of structures would be assigned as follows:

Array Element	Employee_num	Salary
a[0]	1001 - 1002	1003 - 1006
a[1]	1007 - 1008	1009 - 1012
a[2]	1013 - 1014	1015 - 1018

10.6 POINTERS TO STRUCTURE VARIABLES

Just as you can have pointers to characters, integers, and other data types, you can have pointers to structures. This pointer can be made to point to any valid structure, and then contents of that structure's members can be manipulated through this pointer. Take a look at this example. It is the same as the previous example, except that a pointer is used to print the contents of each structure member.

```
//test10_x.cpp
#include <iostream.h>

main()
{
    struct employee
    {
    char employee_num;
    double salary;
    };

    struct employee a[3];  // a[] is an array of structures
    struct employee *ptr;  // ptr to structure of type employee

    a[0].employee_num = 9901;
    a[0].salary = 85000;

    a[1].employee_num = 1026;
    a[1].salary = 66000;

    a[2].employee_num = 3908;
    a[2].salary = 55000;

    cout << "Employee Number  Salary\n "
    for (i=0; i<=2; i++)
    {
        ptr = &a[i];
        cout << ptr->employee_num << " "
            << ptr->salary << "\n";
    }
}
```

The output is:

```
Employee Number  Salary
9901 85000
1026 66000
3908 5000
```

The variable `ptr` is declared as a pointer to a structure of type employee. Next, it is made to point to the first element of the array of structures that are of type employee. Finally, each member of the structure is output through the pointer that was made to point to it. The notation:

```
    ptr->employee_num
```

produces the same output as

```
    a[0].employee_num
```

The -> operator is used to point to or get the value of any structure member. Thus,

- **The syntax for referencing to the contents of a structure member through a pointer is:**

  name_of_pointer->member_name

- **The pointer must be set to the address of a structure before it can be used to reference its contents.**

To complete this section, here is an alternative method of using pointers to structures. The example just presented will be modified to produce the same output:

```cpp
//test10_x.cpp
#include <iostream.h>

main()
{
    struct employee
    {
    char employee_num;
    double salary;
    };

    struct employee a[3];  // a[] is an array of structures
    struct employee *ptr;  // ptr to structure of type employee

    a[0].employee_num = 9901;
    a[0].salary = 85000;

    a[1].employee_num = 1026;
    a[1].salary = 66000;

    a[2].employee_num = 3908;
    a[2].salary = 55000;

    cout << "Employee Number  Salary\n "
    for (ptr=a; ptr<= a+2; ptr++)
    {

        cout << ptr->employee_num << " "
             << ptr->salary << "\n";
    }
}
```

The output is the same as the previous example.

Notice that `ptr` is set to the first element of the array called `a`, which is an array of structures. Recall that the name of the array is actually a pointer to its first element. This is done inside the `for` statement:

```
for (ptr = a;...)
```

The test portion of the `for` statement looks like this:

```
for (...; ptr <= a + 2;...)
```

The loop will execute three times. Recall that

- **Each element of an array can be referenced simply by adding the correct offset to the its name.**

In the first iteration, `ptr` points to the first element of the array. In the second iteration, it is made to point to the second element, and finally the third. The pointer is incremented within the `for` statement:

```
for (...;...;ptr++)
```

The syntax should be quite clear to you by now.

10.7 POINTERS AS STRUCTURE MEMBERS

- **Structure members can be any valid data type.**

You can have characters, integers, floats, and even pointers to any of these data types as structure members. An example will help you understand what has just been said.

```
//test10_x.cpp
#include <iostream.h>

main()
{
    struct course_work
    {
    char course1[20];
    char course2[20];
    struct course_work *ptr;
    }

    // course_work is declared as an array of structures
    course_work semester[3] =
    {{"Computer 101","Math 101",&semester[1];},
     {"Systems 101","Math 102",&semester[2];},
```

```
    {"Analysis 101","Calculus",&semester[0]}};

    int i;

    for (i=0; i<=2; i++)
    {
        cout << "Ptr points to :" << semester[i].ptr << "\n";
    }
}
```

The output for this program is:

```
Pointer points to 0x1ac6
Pointer points to 0x1acc
Pointer points to 0x1ac0
```

In this example, ptr is a member of the structure itself. The structure is declared as an array. Each ptr element of the array is set to point to the address of the next element, execept the last time around, in which case ptr is pointed back to the first element. What you see here is a typical linked list design.

Also, notice that the contents of ptr are output using the standard syntax for structure members:

```
cout << "Ptr points to :" << semester[i].ptr << "\n";
```

Summarizing,

- **Pointers can be structure members, just like any other valid data type.**

- **These pointers follow the same syntax, declaration, and usage rules as pointers which are not structure members.**

- **Structures can contain member pointers to any structure, (not just the structure in which they exist), as long as that structure has been declared.**

We modify the previous program to illustrate how we output the *contents of what ptr is pointing to*, not just the contents of ptr itself.

```
//test10_x.cpp
#include <iostream.h>

main()
{
    struct course_work
    {
    char course1[20];
```

```
char course2[20];
struct course_work *ptr;
}

// course_work is declared as an array of structures
course_work semester[3] =
{{"Computer 101","Math 101",&semester[1];},
  {"Systems 101","Math 102",&semester[2];},
  {"Analysis 101","Calculus",&semester[0]}};

int i;

for (i=0; i<=2; i++)
{
    cout << "Contents being pointed to :"
         << semester[i].ptr->course1 << "\n";
}
}
```

The output for this program is:

```
Contents being pointed to :Systems 101
Contents being pointed to :Analysis 101
Contents being pointed to :Computer 101
```

Notice the syntax used in the cout statement:

```
cout << "Contents being pointed to :"
     << semester[i].ptr->course1 << "\n";
```

Since ptr is a member of a structure, it has to be referenced using that syntax. The contents of what a pointer points to is output using the -> operator, and we follow this operator with the structure member name whose contents are to be displayed.

Take a few moments now to absorb what has just been said; this kind of syntax is frequently used in C++ program.

10.8 STRUCTURES AS STRUCTURE MEMBERS

In the previous section we said that pointers can be any valid data type. Well, a structure is perfectly valid data type. Therefore,

■ **Structures can also exist as individual members within other structures.**

Here's an example:

```
//test10_x.cpp
#include <iostream.h>

main()
{
    struct children
    {
    char boy[10];
    char girl[10];
    };

    struct family
    {
    char husband[10];
    char wife[10];
    struct children Kenneth; // a structure is structure member
    };

    struct children Kenneth = {"Jeff","Sally"};
    struct family Krieger = {"Gene","Sara","Jack","Jill"};

    cout << "Krieger.Kenneth.boy: "
        << Krieger.Kenneth.boy << "\n";
    cout << "Krieger.Kenneth.girl: "
        << Krieger.Kenneth.girl << "\n";
}
```

The output for this program is:

```
Krieger.Kenneth.boy: Jack
Krieger.Kenneth.girl: Jill
```

This example illustrates how a structure can exist as a structure member within another structure. Notice the syntax for referencing this member:

```
Krieger.Kenneth.boy
```

The name of the outermost structure is followed by the next one in line, and so on. Kenneth is a structure member of Krieger; hence, Krieger will precede Kenneth. If one of the members of the structure children was also a structure, called, say description, then any member of that structure member (say height), would have been referenced like this:

```
Kenneth.Krieger.Description.height
```

We can safely conclude the following:

- **Structures can exist as structure members within other structures.**

- **Structures can be embedded to the level that your compiler or computer supports.**

- **All structures, whether embedded or not, must be defined somewhere in the program.**

10.9 MODIFYING STRUCTURES INSIDE FUNCTIONS

Structures or any of its members can be passed to and from functions. The rules for modifying structures inside functions are the same as that of any other data type:

- **Contents of structure members can be modified indirectly, through a pointer.**

This is because copies of variables are sent to functions in the form of arguments, not the actual variables. Pointers can be set to the addresses of structure members, and then sent as arguments to functions. Here's an example that illustrates what has just been said.

```
//test10_x.cpp
#include <iostream.h>

struct couple
   {
   char man[];
   char woman[];
   }

void break_up(struct couple *ptr);
main()
{
   struct couple Camastra = {"John","Sara"};
   struct couple *ptr;

   ptr = &Camastra;

   cout << "Before break_up, Camastra couple was: \n";
   cout << Camastra.man << " " << Camastra.woman << "\n";

   break_up(ptr);

   cout << "After break_up, Camastra couple is: \n";
   cout << Camastra.man << " " << Camastra.woman << "\n";
```

```
}

void break_up(struct couple *ptr)
{
    ptr->woman = 'C';
}
```

This program illustrates the classic case of a break up. The output is:

```
Before break-up, Camastra couple was:
John Sara
After break-up, Camastra couple is:
John Cara
```

It also illustrates how the contents of structure members can be modified inside functions via pointers to them.

10.10 REVIEW

In this chapter, we understood the concept of a structure and how it is represented in C++. A structure groups together, in a fixed pattern, different pieces of information, and gives it a name. We learned how to assign values to structure members. We also learned:

- How arrays of structures are declared and stored in a computer

- How pointers to structure variables are used

- How pointers to structures can be structure members as well

- How structure members can be modified inside functions via pointers

The Power of C++

11

The Class Mechanism

11.1 INTRODUCTION

Starting with this chapter, we now present those features of C++ that make it the powerful language that it is. We start with a discussion of one of the key concepts in C++: the class mechanism. Not only will you understand how to declare, define, and use classes, but, more importantly, you will learn the reason for using a class as opposed to a structure, and the advantages in doing so. In the next chapter, rules specific to class member declarations and definitions will be discussed.

We start with a review of structures, which were discussed in detail in the previous chapter.

11.2 STRUCTURES IN C++

As discussed in the previous chapter, a structure is a special data type that gathers together, in a fixed pattern, other valid data types. Here's a simple structure declaration:

```
struct family
    {
    char *husband;
    char *wife;
    char *son;
    char *daughter;
    };
struct family Anderson;
```

The structure `family` comprises four variables which are pointers to character arrays. These variables are called husband, wife, son, and daughter, respectively. Anderson is a structure of type `family`. The members of Anderson can also be initialized at the time they are declared, and accessed through a pointer:

```
Anderson.husband = "John Anderson";
Anderson.wife = "Mary Anderson";
Anderson.son = "Joey Anderson";
Anderson.daughter = "Marla Anderson";
```

The members of Anderson can be accessed through a pointer, as illustrated in the following program:

```
// test11_1.cpp

#include    <iostream.h>

struct family
    {
    char *husband;
    char *wife;
    char *son;
    char *daughter;
    };

// Anderson is declared as a structure of type family
// notice that keyword struct or structure is missing
family Anderson =
    {{"John Anderson"}, {"Mary Anderson"},
     {"Joey Anderson"}, {"Marla Anderson"}};

// ptr points to structur of type family
family *ptr;

main(void)
{
    // ptr points to 1st member of Anderson
    ptr = &Anderson;

    cout <<"husband is  " << ptr->husband <<"\n"
    <<"wife is     " << ptr->wife    <<"\n"
    <<"son is      " << ptr->son     <<"\n"
    <<"daughter is " << ptr->daughter<<"\n";
}
```

Compiling and running this program will result in the following output:

```
husband is John Anderson
wife is Mary Anderson
son is Joey Anderson
```

```
daughter is Marla Anderson
```

A structure with a tag-name of family is declared, Anderson is defined as a structure of this type, and the members are initialized. Next, ptr is declared as a pointer to structures of that type. Inside main(), ptr is set to point to the location in memory where the structure Anderson is stored. The structure members of Anderson are printed through a cout() statement, using ptr to point to the correct member.

Notice that the keyword struct (or structure) is missing when Anderson and ptr are declared. In C++, this keyword is optional. However, it is not optional when the structure template is declared.

If you take another look at main(), you will realize that it can perhaps be logically divided into two parts. The first part initializes ptr to point to the structure Anderson. The second part simply outputs the contents of each member. Since functions are used to divide a program into its logical components, where each function performs a coherent task on its own, let's modify test11_1.cpp and create two functions to do the job:

```cpp
// test11_2.cpp

#include <iostream.h>

struct family
    {
    char *husband;
    char *wife;
    char *son;
    char *daughter;
    };

family Anderson =
    {{"John Anderson"}, {"Mary Anderson"},
     {"Joey Anderson"}, {"Marla Anderson"}};

// ptr points to structure of type family
family *ptr;

// function prototypes follow
family  *initialize(family *ptr);
void output(family *ptr);

main(void)
    {
    // set pointer to initialize()
    // send ptr to output()
    ptr = initialize(ptr);
    output(ptr);
    }

family *initialize(family *ptr)
    {
```

```
    ptr = &Anderson;
    return ptr;
}

void output(family *ptr)
{
    cout <<"husband is " << ptr->husband <<"\n"
        <<"wife is " << ptr->wife      <<"\n"
        <<"son is " << ptr->son        <<"\n"
        <<"daughter is " << ptr->daughter<<"\n";
}
```

The output for this program looks like this:

```
husband is John Anderson
wife is Mary Anderson
son is Joey Anderson
daughter is Marla Anderson
```

Now assume that 1000 lines of code, comprising, say, 15 additional functions, are added to the original program. The calls to these additional functions are made from main(). The program would look something like this:

```
// test11_3.cpp

#include    <iostream.h>

struct family
    {
    char *husband;
    char *wife;
    char *son;
    char *daughter;
    };
family Anderson;

family Anderson =
    {{"John Anderson"}, {"Mary Anderson"},
     {"Joey Anderson"}, {"Marla Anderson"}};

// ptr points to structure of type family
family *ptr;

// function prototypes follow
family  *initialize(family *ptr);
void output(family *ptr);

// function prototypes for the 15 additional functions are
// added  here......

main(void)
{
```

```
    // ptr receives pointer to Anderson
    ptr = initialize(ptr);

    // Calls to the 15 additional functions are made here
    output(ptr);
}

// The code for function initialize() is stil the same
family *initialize(family *ptr)
{
    ptr = &Anderson;
    return ptr;
}

// Code for 15 additional functions is over here.....
// The code for function output() is still the same
void output(family *ptr)
{
    cout <<"husband is " << ptr->husband <<"\n"
        <<"wife is " << ptr->wife     <<"\n"
        <<"son is " << ptr->son       <<"\n"
        <<"daughter is " << ptr->daughter<<"\n";
}
```

Suppose this program produces the following output:

```
husband is Mark Davis
wife is Jennifer Davis
son is Michael Davis
daughter is Maria Davis
```

On verification of the output, it appears that somewhere in the course of the program, ptr has been erroneously made to point to some other structure of type family, (perhaps called Davis), and its structure members have been initialized to the member names of the Davis family. What this means for you as a programmer is many hours of headache and wasted time, tracing through the 1000 line program, trying to locate the function in which ptr was reset to point to the location in memory of the Davis family, instead of Anderson. This is where C++ comes to the rescue.

11.3 THE CLASS MECHANISM IN C++

C++ has a class mechanism that allows you to specify a unique set of objects which comprise that class, and the operations allowed on these objects. Let's modify the original version of the program (test11_2.cpp) to use a class instead of a structure, and see how classes work.

```
//    test_4.cpp

#include <iostream.h>
class family
    {
    // notice use of keyword private
    // member list follows this keyword
    // ptr is declared inside family
    private:
    char *husband;
    char *wife;
    char *son;
    char *daughter;
    family *ptr;

    // notice use of keyword public
    // member functions follow this keyword
    public:
    void initialize(void);
    void output(family *ptr);
    };

// Anderson is object of type family
family Anderson;

main(void)
{
    // initialize() is qualified by class object name.
    // notice the dot operator.
    Anderson.initialize();
}
// initialize() is qualified by class name
void family::initialize(void)
{
    // initializing member list of object Anderson
    // class members are qualified by class object name
    Anderson.ptr = &Anderson;
    Anderson.ptr->husband = "John Anderson";
    Anderson.ptr->wife = "Mary Anderson";
    Anderson.ptr->son = "Joey Anderson";
    Anderson.ptr->daughter = "Marla Anderson";
    Anderson.output(Anderson.ptr);
}

// output() is qualified by class name
void family::output(family *ptr)
{
    cout <<"husband is " << ptr->husband    <<"\n"
         <<"wife is " << ptr->wife         <<"\n"
         <<"son is " << ptr->son           <<"\n"
         <<"daughter is " << ptr->daughter  <<"\n";
}
```

This program produces the following output:

```
husband is John Anderson
wife is Mary Anderson
son is Joey Anderson
daughter is Marla Anderson
```

Now let's step through this program and understand why a class was used instead of a structure, and why it was declared that way.

The keyword class is followed by the class tagname, called family, (just like a structure tagname in C), and then an opening curly brace (once again, like C structure declarations). What this does is create a unique type, a class type called family.

Next, you see the keyword private, followed by a colon, and then a list of declarations. The list of declarations that are enclosed within the opening and closing curly braces within a class declaration is known as the *member list*. The keyword private is an access specifier, which indicates access privileges for the declarations that follow it. This keyword specifies that the variables that follow can be used only by the member functions that exist within that class (or its *friends*, but we will postpone discussion of the friend mechanism to a later chapter). But what are member functions? Let's continue to analyze the declaration before we answer that question.

Following the keyword private are the declarations for husband, wife, son, daughter. Then, there is one for family *ptr. husband, wife, son, and daughter are called class members (just like structure members). ptr is declared to be a pointer to a class of type family. Notice that the keyword class does not precede the class tag-name family, just as struct is not required to precede the declaration of a structure of that type. The compiler understands that family is a class name, because it was specified as such at the beginning of the class declaration.

Next is the keyword public, followed by a colon, and a list of function declarations. These functions are called *member functions*, or *methods*. Since these functions are declared as public, they can be accessed by members of their class as well as nonmembers. They can be passed arguments and accessed from anywhere within program scope.

Inside main(), there is a function call to the class member function initialize(). Notice that this function is prefixed with Anderson, and a dot (.). Recall how structure members are accessed:

```
struct family
    {
    char *husband;
    char *wife;
    char *son;
    char *daughter;
    };
struct family Anderson;
```

```
Anderson.husband = "John Anderson";
Anderson.wife   = "Mary Anderson";
Anderson.son = "Joey Anderson";
Anderson.daughter = "Marla Anderson";
```

The structure members are prefixed with the name given to structures of that type and the dot operator.

Class members are referenced the same way. `initialize()` is a member function of the class `family`, and `Anderson` is an object of that type. A function call to `initialize()` is as follows:

```
Anderson.initialize();
```

Now take a look at the function definition of `initialize()`:

```
void family::initialize(void)
{
      .
      .
```

Notice that the function name is preceded by the class name and scope resolution operator `::`. Recall from Part 1 of the book how C++ allows different functions to have the same name. It is possible that there may be other functions in our program that have the name `initialize()`. However, the compiler understands this to be a member function of the class `family` simply because it is preceded with the class name! To say it a little bit differently, this function is qualified by a class name. Now you should be able to understand why `::` is called the scope resolution operator; it resolves the scope of the function name that it precedes, it allows the compiler to understand whether the function definition that follows belongs to a class or structure, or is simply an independent entity on its own. Let's continue with the code:

```
Anderson.ptr = &Anderson;
Anderson.ptr->husband = "John Anderson";
Anderson.ptr->wife = "Mary Anderson";
Anderson.ptr->son = "Joey Anderson";
Anderson.ptr->daughter = "Marla Anderson";
Anderson.output(Anderson.ptr);
```

The class member `ptr` is assigned the location in memory of the class object name `Anderson`. Then, the remaining members are initialized. Finally, the function member `output()` is called and this call is also qualified by the class object name.

The program ends with a definition of the function `output()`. This function is also qualified by class name. The return value and type and number of arguments agree with the class declaration.

Summarizing,

- **Classes are declared via the keyword** class.

- **Classes, like structures, have tagnames.** **The tagname** family **is assigned to the class in the sample program.**

- **A class comprises a list of declarations of variables** *and/or functions*.

  Our class member list comprises the pointers to character arrays called husband, wife, son, and daughter, respectively. In addition to this, ptr is declared as a pointer to a class of type family. The functions initialize() and output() are the member functions in the class member list.

- **The keyword** *class* **does not have to precede the declaration of variables that are objects or instances of that type.**

  In the sample program, Anderson is an object or an instance of a class of type family.

- **Access specifiers, such as** private **and** public, **are used to specify access privileges of the member list within the class.**

  In the program, the class members husband, wife, son, daughter, and ptr are private. The member functions initialize() and output() are public. What this means is that any valid argument can be passed to initialize() and output() from anywhere within the program. However, the private class members can be accessed by the functions initialize() and output() only. To reiterate, husband, wife, son, daughter, and ptr can be assigned values or manipulated through the functions initialize() and output() only.

- **Member function calls are qualified by the class object name and the dot operator.**

- **Member function definitions are qualified by the class name and the scope resolution operator.**

- **The return value type, function name, and number and type of arguments of a member function must agree with its corresponding declaration within the class.**

So why bother with classes anyway? Let's go back to the scenario that was presented in test11_3.cpp. In that program, ptr had somehow been erroneously set to point to the location in memory of the Davis family structure. The problem was that you as a programmer had to sift through 1000 lines of code comprising more than 15 functions to figure out where ptr had been reset. However, if 1000 lines of code were added to test11_4.cpp, and something were to go wrong, you could narrow down your search to two functions only: initialize() and output(). This is because the variables that have the incorrect value in them were specified as private members of a class, which means that they could be manipulated by these two functions only.

Thus,

- *A class mechanism allows you to group together variables and functions that can be performed on these variables as a single and unique type.*

- **Classes also allow you to** *localize problems quickly*, **through the access privileges specified within the class declaration.**

In addition to this, suppose you were required to modify the program at a later date, and the modifications pertained to the members of the class family only. Given that these members are declared as private, all you have to do is modify the logic within the two functions that are the member functions of this class. Just think of the ease of maintenance of such programs, think of the power that is placed at your fingertips!

11.4 SOME COMMON ERRORS

Now that you understand the fundamental concept of classes, a few variations will be made to test11_4.cpp to see how the compiler responds to these changes. main() will be modified to qualify initialize() by class name, instead of class object name. All subsequent changes to the original program will be highlighted by imbedding a double asterisk within the comment. Make sure you pay special attention to these changes.

```
//     test11_5.cpp

#include <iostream.h>

class family
    {
    // notice use of keyword private
```

```
    // member list follows this keyword
    // ptr is declared inside family
    private:
    char *husband;
    char *wife;
    char *son;
    char *daughter;
    family *ptr;

    // notice use of keyword public
    // member functions follow this keyword
    public:
    void initialize(void);
    void output(family *ptr);
    };

// Anderson is object of type family
family Anderson;

main(void)
{
// ** initialize() is qualified by class name only
family::initialize();
}

// initialize() is qualified by class name
void family::initialize(void)
{
    // initializing member list of object Anderson
    // class members are qualified by class object name
    Anderson.ptr = &Anderson;
    Anderson.ptr->husband = "John Anderson";
    Anderson.ptr->wife = "Mary Anderson";
    Anderson.ptr->son = "Joey Anderson";
    Anderson.ptr->daughter = "Marla Anderson";
    Anderson.output(Anderson.ptr);
}

// output() is qualified by class name
void family::output(family *ptr)
{
    cout << "husband is " << ptr->husband << "\n"
    << "wife is " << ptr->wife << "\n"
    << "son is " << ptr->son << "\n"
    << "daughter is " << ptr->daughter << "\n";
}
```

Compiling this program results in the following unfriendly message from the compiler:

```
Error:  Use . or -> to call family::initialize()
```

The declaration

```
family Anderson;
```

could just as well have been a declaration such as this:

```
family Anderson, Davis, Samuel;
```

    The compiler needs to know which one of these objects or instances is being operated on. That is why it is necessary to prefix the object name that is being operated in the function call in `main()`. Thus, the statement `family::initialize` is incorrect.

    Summarizing,

■ **You must prefix the call to** `classes` **with the class instance name, not the class name.**

    Now let's modify the original version (`test11_4.cpp`) and reference the class members in the function `initialize()` without qualifying them by any name at all. Remember, the changes are highlighted by a double asterisk within the comment.

```
//    test11_6.cpp

#include <iostream.h>

class family
    {
    // notice use of keyword private
    // member list follows private declaration
    private:
    char *husband;
    char *wife;
    char *son;
    char *daughter;
    family *ptr;

    // notice use of keyword public
    // member functions follow this keyword
    public:
    void initialize(void);
    void output(family *ptr);
    };

// Anderson is object of type family
family Anderson;

main(void)
{
    // initialize() is qualified by class object name.
    Anderson.initialize();
}
```

```
// initialize() is qualified by class name
void family::initialize(void)
{
    // initializing member list of object Anderson
    // ** class members are not qualified by class object name
    ptr = &Anderson;
    ptr->husband = "John Anderson";
    ptr->wife = "Mary Anderson";
    ptr->son = "Joey Anderson";
    ptr->daughter = "Marla Anderson";
    output(ptr);
}

// output() is qualified by class name
void family::output(family *ptr)
{
    cout << "husband is " << ptr->husband << "\n"
    << "wife is " << ptr->wife << "\n"
    << "son is " << ptr->son << "\n"
    << "daughter is " << ptr->daughter << "\n";
}
```

When this program is compiled, (much to our amazement) there are no errors. The output is the same as for test11_6.cpp. Let's see why.

ptr is set to the location in memory of the object Anderson. Hence, each time ptr is used to initialize members of the class, the object Anderson is being operated on. That is why there is no need to qualify ptr by object name; the compiler understands.

Let's modify the original version again, and try to initialize ptr in main(). ptr will be sent as an actual argument to initialize(), and the class declaration and function definitions will be modified accordingly.

```
//    test11_7.cpp

#include <iostream.h>

class family
    {
    // notice use of keyword private
    // member list follows private declaration
    private:
    char *husband;
    char *wife;
    char *son;
    char *daughter;
    family *ptr;

    // notice use of keyword public
    // ** ptr is sent as an argument to initialize()
    public:
    void initialize(family *ptr);
    void output(family *ptr);
```

```
    };

// Anderson is object of type family
family Anderson;

main(void)
{
    // ** accessing private member in main()
    Anderson.ptr = &Anderson;

    // ** send ptr to initialize()
    Anderson.initialize(Anderson.ptr);
}

// ** initialize() receives ptr as argument
void family::initialize(family *ptr)
{
    // initializing member list of object Anderson
    // class members are not qualified by class object name
    ptr->husband = "John Anderson";
    ptr->wife = "Mary Anderson";
    ptr->son = "Joey Anderson";
    ptr->daughter = "Marla Anderson";
    output(ptr);
}

// output() is qualified by class name
void family::output(family *ptr)
{
    cout << "husband is " << ptr->husband << "\n"
    << "wife is " << ptr->wife << "\n"
    <<"son is " << ptr->son << "\n"
    <<"daughter is " << ptr->daughter<< "\n";
}
```

Compiling this program results in the following message:

```
Error:   family::ptr is not accessible
```

The reason for this message should be obvious, if you take a moment to think of what happened. ptr is declared as a private member of the class family. Summarizing,

- **Private members of classes can be manipulated only by its class member functions.**

Let's try one more variation to the original program before closing this chapter. This time the function prototypes of initialize() and output() will be declared outside the class declaration.

```
//    test11_8.cpp

#include <iostream.h>
class family
    {
    // notice use of keyword private
    // member list follows private declaration
    private:
    char *husband;
    char *wife;
    char *son;
    char *daughter;
    family *ptr;

    // notice use of keyword public
    // member functions follow
    public:
    void initialize(void);
    void output(family *ptr);
    };

// Anderson is object of type family
family Anderson;

// ** function prototypes of class members functions follow
void initialize(void);
void output(family *ptr);

main(void)
{
    // initialize() is qualified by class object name
    Anderson.initialize();
}

// initialize() is qualified by class name
void family::initialize(void)
{
    // initializing member list of object Anderson
    // class members are not qualified by class object name
    ptr->husband = "John Anderson";
    ptr->wife = "Mary Anderson";
    ptr->son = "Joey Anderson";
    ptr->daughter = "Marla Anderson";
    output(ptr);
}

// output() is qualified by class name
void family::output(family *ptr)
{
    cout << "husband is " << ptr->husband << "\n"
    << "wife is " << ptr->wife << "\n"
    << "son is " << ptr->son << "\n"
    <<" daughter is " << ptr->daughter << "\n";
}
```

Compiling this program results in the following messages:

```
Error:
Class member 'initialize' declared outside its class
Class member 'output' declared outside its class
```

The compiler matched the return value, function name, and type and number of arguments of each function prototype with the declarations inside the class. Since it found the declarations of its member functions outside the class definition, this error message was issued.

Summarizing,

- **Member functions cannot be redeclared anywhere except within their class.**

If any of the factors had not matched, the compiler would not have issued this message. For example, the following declarations would have been acceptable:

```
void initialize(int i, int j);
void output(int k, char l);
```

However, declarations such as these would have the compiler believe that these functions do not belong to any class or structure. It would expect to find two sets of definitions each for both initialize() and output(). The set that belongs to the class would be prefixed by the class name and scope resolution operator, as we have illustrated in previous programs. The set that does not belong to the class would simply be defined as is:

```
        .
        .
void initialize(int i, int j)
{
        .
        .
}
void output(int k, char l)
{
        .
        .
}
```

11.5 REVIEW

Let's summarize what we have learned in this chapter:

- Classes offer a mechanism for grouping together variables and functions that can be performed on those variables within a single unique type.

- Classes allow quick localization of problems and ease of maintenance of programs.

- The member list within a class comprises variable declarations and, optionally, member functions.

- Public member function calls are prefixed with the class object name.

- Member function definitions are prefixed with the class name and the scope resolution operator.

- Member functions within a class cannot be redeclared outside their classes.

Scope and Member Access of Classes

12.1 INTRODUCTION

Rules specific to classes, class members and member functions will be discussed in this chapter. If you understand the fundamental concepts described in the previous chapter, you should be able to breeze quickly through this one. If you are not comfortable yet, then this chapter should help in achieving that end. Some of the information here may seem redundant, but this will help reinforce the ideas introduced in previous chapters. It is essential that you understand classes completely in order to recognize their full potential and power.

12.2 CLASS DECLARATIONS

■ **Classes are declared as follows:**

```
class class_name
    {
    // member list follows
    // member functions are also known as methods
    member_1;
    member_2;
    member_3;
    member_function_1();
    member_function_2();
    };
```

■ *Objects* or *instances* of classes are defined as follows:

```
// instance_1 is an instance of class type class_name
class_name instance_1;
```

12.3 CLASS NAME SCOPE

■ **Class name has to be unique within its scope.**

You cannot assign the same class name to two different types of classes. Take a look at the following program:

```
//     test12_1.cpp

#include <iostream.h>

class increment
    {
    // public member list follows
    public:
    int i;
    int j;
    int add_one(int i, int j);
    };

class increment      // ERROR! SAME CLASS NAME
    {
    // public member list follows
    public:
    int k;
    int sub_one(int k);
    };

// var1 is an instance of class increment
// var2 is an instance of class increment
increment var1;
increment var2;

main(void)
{
    // x and y are local to main()
    int x, y;

    // initialize class members of object var1
    var1.i = 1;
    var1.j = 2;

    x = var1.add_one(var1.i, var1.j);

    // initialize class members of object var2
    var2.k = 5;

    y = var2.sub_one(var2.k);
    cout << "x is " << x << " \n"
```

```
            "y is " << y << " \n";
}

// add_one is qualified by class name
int increment::add_one(int i, int j)
{
   int l;
   l = i + j;
   return l;
}

// sub_one is qualified by class name
int increment::sub_one(int k)
{
   k -= 1;
   return k;
}
```

Compiling this program results in this error:

```
Error:  Multiple declaration for increment()
```

The problem can be fixed by changing one of the class names, as follows:

```
//     test12_2.cpp

#include <iostream.h>

class increment
   {
   // public member list follows
   public:
   int i;
   int j;
   int add_one(int i, int j);
   };

// ** Notice different class name
class decrement
   {
   // public member list follows
   public:
   int k;
   int sub_one(int k);
   };

increment var1;     // var1 is an instance of class increment
decrement var2;     // var2 is an instance of class decrement

main(void)
{
   // x and y are local to main()
```

```
    int x, y;

    // class members of object var1 are initialized
    var1.i = 1;
    var1.j = 2;

    x = var1.add_one(var1.i, var1.j);

    // class member of var2 are initialized
    var2.k = 5;

    y = var2.sub_one(var2.k);
    cout << "x is " << x << " \n"
         "y is " << y << " \n";
}

// add_one is qualified by class name
int increment::add_one(int i, int j)
{
    int l;
    l = i + j;
    return l;
}

// sub_one is qualified by class name
int decrement::sub_one(int k)
{
    k -= 1;
    return k;
}
```

Compiling and running this program will result in the following output:

```
x is 3
y is 4
```

Now take a look at this program, in which two classes are assigned the same name:

```
//    test12_3.cpp

#include <iostream.h>

class increment
    {
    // public member list follows
    public:
    int i;
    int j;
    int add_one(int i, int j);
    };
```

```
// var1 is an instance of class increment
increment var1;


// function prototype follows
int sub_one(int y);

main(void)
{
    // x and y are local to main()
     int x, y;

    // class members of object var1 are initialized
     var1.i = 1;
     var1.j = 2;

     x = var1.add_one(var1.i, var1.j);

     y = sub_one(y);

     cout << "x is " << x << " \n"
        << "y is " << y << " \n";
}
// add_one is qualified by class name
int increment::add_one(int i, int j)
{
     int l;
     l = i + j;
     return l;
}

// sub_one is not qualified by class name
int sub_one(int k)
{
// ** Notice same class name
class increment
     {
     public:
     int k;
     };

// var2 is an object of type class increment
increment var2;

// member of class increment is initialized
var2.k = 5;
return var2.k;
}
```

This program produces the following output:

```
x is 3
y is 5
```

This version worked, even though two class names (increment) were assigned the same name.   The reason for this is because the second declaration of the class increment() is out of scope of the first declaration.   So what is the scope of a class name? It starts at the point of declaration and ends at the end of the enclosing block.   Summarizing,

- **Two classes of the same name will be correctly recognized by the compiler, as long as they are not within scope of each other.**

In the sample program, the second declaration of increment() is within the function sub_one, which is out of scope of the first declaration of increment().

12.4 CLASS MEMBER DATA TYPES

- **The class member list can comprise any valid C++ data type.**

It can contain the usual primary types:

```
class primary
    {
    int a;     // integer
    char b;    // character
    float c;   // float
    double d;  // double
    };
// class_1 is an object of type primary
primary class_1;
```

It can contain structures:

```
class structure_1
    {
    // member list contains structure of type family
    struct family;
    };
// Anderson is object of type structure_1
structure_1 Anderson
```

It can contain pointers to any valid type:

```
class pointer_1
    {
    // ptr is pointer to structure of type family
    struct family;
    struct family *ptr;
```

```
};
```

```
// Anderson is an object of type pointer_1
pointer_1 Anderson;
```

It can even contain classes. However, the class inside a class must have been previously declared elsewhere.
Take a look at the following program:

```
//    test12_4.cpp

#include <iostream.h>

class class_2
   {
   public:
   int i;
   };

class class_1
   {
   public:
   int j;

   // variable_2 is a nested class
   class_2 variable_2;
   };

// variable_1 is an object of type class_1
class_1 variable_1;

main(void)
{
   variable_1.variable_2.i = 12;
   cout << "i is " << variable_1.variable_2.i << "\n";
}
```

This program gives the following output:

```
i is 12
```

This program worked because class_2 is defined, and then it is declared as a class member of class_1. Notice the syntax for accessing a member of a nested class:

```
variable_1.variable_2.i
```

- **The rule for accessing members of nested classes is to start with the object name of the outermost class, and then work your way to the class that is being accessed.**

Now look at what happens if the declaration of class_1 is moved below class_2:

```
//    test12_5.cpp

#include <iostream.h>

class class_1
     {
     public:
     int j;

   // variable_2 is a nested class
     class_2 variable_2;
     };

// variable_1 is an object of type class_1
class_1 variable_1;

// class_2 is declared after class_1 references it
class class_2
     {
     public:
     int i;
     };

main(void)
{
     variable_1.variable_2.i = 12;
     cout << "i is " << variable_1.variable_2.i << "\n";
}
```

Compiling this version results in the following message:

```
Error:   Type name expected
```

This is because the class class_2 is declared inside class_1, but class_2 has not been defined yet.

12.5 CLASS MEMBER STORAGE SPECIFIERS

- **The class member list declarations can be preceded with any storage class specifier except** auto, extern, **and** register.

A class declared this way:

```
class invalid_1
     {
     // invalid storage class specifiers follow:
     auto int a;
```

```
    extern char b;
    register int c;
    };
```

```
// variable is object of type invalid_1
invalid_1 variable;
```

will cause the compiler to generate the following messages:

```
Error:   Storage class 'auto' not allowed for a field
Error:   Storage class 'extern' not allowed for a field
Error:   Storage class 'register' not allowed for a field
```

12.5.1 Static Class Members

Take a look at this class declaration:

```
class add_1
    {
    int counter;
    int i;
    int add_number(int);
    };
```

The declaration above declares a class called add_1, which contains declarations for two integers and one function. When several variables of that class type are declared, for example,

```
add_1 class_1, class_2, class_3;
```

copies of the data members of add_1 are assigned to each. That is, class_1, class_2, and class_3 will each be a class of type add_1.

Now suppose that the value of counter is the same for all variables. (Perhaps counter counts the number of times a loop is entered). For the duration of the program, three copies of this value will exist, when, in fact, it would be more efficient to have just one. C++ allows us to get around situations such as these by allowing the keyword static to precede the declaration of that specific type.

Static implies that there will be only one copy of the type declared as such, and it will be shared by all data objects or instances of that type. Now look at the following declaration:

```
class add_1
    {
    private:

    // notice keyword static
    static int counter;
```

```
public:
int i;
int add_number(int);
};
```

The keyword static precedes the declaration of counter. Now when objects of this class are declared:

```
add_1 class_1, class_2, class_3;
```

the location in memory for their static member counter will be the same.

This is more efficient, since there is only one copy of the member and its contents will not vary for each instance of that type.

The advantages offered by static members can now be summarized:

■ They reduce the need for global variables.

■ They make obvious which data can be logically shared within a class.

12.6 CLASS MEMBER ACCESS SPECIFIERS

You should be able to read through this section rapidly, since it mainly reinforces concepts that you have already read about and seen extensively in previous programs.

■ **Class members can be made** public, private, **or** protected.

Within a class declaration, each one of these keywords can be used to precede one or more class member declarations. The class members acquire special characteristics, based on their access specifier.

12.6.1 Public Access

■ **In C++, all members of a structure are** public **by default.**

In the declaration below:

```
struct familiy
   {
   char *husband;
   char *wife;
   char *son;
   char *daughter;
   };
```

```
// Anderson is structure of type family
family Anderson;
```

the structure members husband, wife, son, and daughter can be accessed
from anywhere within the program.

- **Class members are** `private` **by default.**

    All public members must be specified explicitly.

```
class family
    {
    // public class members follow
    public:
    char *husband;
    char *wife;
    char *son;
    char *daughter;
    };
```

```
// Anderson is class of type family
family Anderson;
```

- **An access modifier remains effective for all declarations that**
  follow it, until a different access modifier is encountered. The
  modifier can be reinserted more than once.

    The following declaration is valid:

```
class family
    {
    // public class members follow
    public:
    char *husband;
    char *wife;

    // private class members follow
    private:
    char *son;
    char *daughter;

    // class members that follow are public again
    public:
    char *neice;
    };
```

Here's a short program that illustrates the use of public class
members:

```
//    test12_6.cpp
```

```
#include <iostream.h>

void function_1(int i);

class add_numbers
    {
    // public class members follow
    public:
    int i;
    int add_sum(int);
    };

// one is an object of type add_numbers
add_numbers one;

main(void)
{
    one.i = 1;
    function_1(one.i);
}


void function_1(int i)
{
    i += 5;
    cout << "i is " << i << "\n";
}
```

The output is:

```
i is 6
```

Notice that function_1() is not a member function of the class add_numbers. Yet the compiler allowed it to take i as an argument and change its value. This is because i was declared as public, and therefore there are no access restrictions on it.

12.6.2 Private Access

■ **In C++, all member declarations are** private **by default.**

Thus, the following declaration:

```
class family
    {
    char *husband;
    char *wife;
    char *son;
    char *daughter;
    };
```

is equivalent to

```
class family
    {
    private:
    char *husband;
    char *wife;
    char *son;
    char *daughter;
    };
```

- **Private members can be accessed by their class member functions only (and by *friends* of a class, a topic that we will discuss later on in this chapter).**

Here's another version of test12_6.cpp, which specifies its class members as private instead of public:

```
//    test12_7.cpp

#include <iostream.h>

void function_1(int i);

class add_numbers
    {
    // class members are private by default
    int i;
    int add_sum(int);
    };

// one is an object of type add_numbers
add_numbers one;

main(void)
{
    one.i = 1;
    function_1(one.i);
}

void function_1(int i)
{
    i += 5;
    cout << "i is " << i << "\n";
}
```

Compiling this version gives an error:

```
Error:   add_numbers::i is not accessible
```

This error is caused by a call to function_1() inside main(), in which an argument of type integer is being sent. However, the integer that is being sent happens to be a private member of the class add_numbers, and function_1() does not have access privileges to it because it is not a member (or friend) function.

Let's modify test12_7.cpp to see what would happen if some other variable is sent to function_1(). We will send the variable k, which is initialized in main().

```cpp
//    test12_8.cpp

#include <iostream.h>

void function_1(int i);

class add_numbers
    {
    // class members are private by default
    int i;
    int add_num(int);
    };

// one is an object of type add_numbers
add_numbers one;
main(void)
{
    // k is local to main()
    // k is sent as an argument to function_1()
    int k = 10;
    function_1(k);
}

void function_1(int k)
{
    k += 5;
    cout << "k is " << k << "\n";
}
```

This program compiles correctly, and results in the following output:

```
k is 15
```

The reason for this is simple. The variable k is declared within main(), it is not a class member, and therefore it has no access restrictions. Hence, it can be sent as an argument to function_1(), which is also not a class member.

Now let's try to send the class member i to its class member function add_num():

```cpp
//    test12_9.cpp

#include <iostream.h>
```

```
void function_1(int i);

class add_numbers
    {
    // class members are private by default
    int i;
    void add_num(void);
    };

// one is an object of type add_numbers
add_numbers one;

main(void)
{
    // k is local to main()
    // k is sent as argument to function_1()
    int k = 10;
    function_1(k);

    // add_num() is called
    one.add_num();

}
void function_1(int k)
{
    k += 5;
    cout << "k is " << k << "\n";
}

void add_numbers::add_num(void)
{
    one.i = 5;
    cout << "i is " << one.i << "\n";
}
```

Compiling this program results in the following message:

```
Error:   add_numbers::add_num is not accessible
```

The reason for this message is obvious. add_num is a private member
of its class, and therefore not accessible from main(). So how can
add_num() be accessed? It is common (and logical) to declare data
members of a class as private and member functions as public. The
majority of class declarations in C++ programs are declared in this way.
Doing so to test12_9.cpp will fix the problem:

```
class add_numbers
    {
    // class members are private by default
    // class method is public
    int i;
    public:
```

```
void add_num(void);
};
```

The output is as follows:

```
k is 15
i is 5
```

12.6.3 Protected Access

Protected access concerns member access by a derived class. But since derived classes have not been discussed yet, a discussion on this topic will be deferred until then.

12.7 CLASS MEMBER FUNCTIONS

- **All functions that are declared within a class are called** *member functions* **or** *methods*.

Member function scope and access rules are the same as regular class members.

12.8 FRIEND FUNCTIONS

- **A class member function name can be prefixed with the keyword** *friend*. **This is a** friend **function.**

Take a look at the following declaration of a friend function:

```
class family
    {
    // private members follow
    private:
    char *husband;
    char *wife;
    char *son;
    char *daughter;
    family *ptr;

    // public members follow
    public:
    void initialize(void);

    // ** notice friend function
    friend void output(family *ptr);
```

```
};
```

A class of type family is declared, with private members husband, wife, son, daughter, and ptr and public function member initialize(). The function output() is prefixed with the keyword friend, thus, this is a friend function.

- **A** friend **function is not a member of that class. However, it has full access to the private and protected members of that class.**

We now illustrate the use of a friend function inside a program. Take a look at a program that uses this class.

```
//    test12_11.cpp

#include <iostream.h>;

class family
    {
    private:
    char *husband;
    char *wife;
    char *son;
    char *daughter;
    family *ptr;
    public:
    void initialize(void);

    // notice friend function
    friend void output(family *ptr);
    };

// Anderson is object of type family
family Anderson;

// ** notice function prototype for output()
void output(family *ptr);

main(void)
{
    Anderson.initialize();
}

// notice class name and scope resolution operator
void family::initialize(void)
{
    Anderson.ptr = &Anderson;
    ptr->husband =  "John Anderson";
    ptr->wife    =  "Mary Anderson";
    ptr->son     =  "Joey Anderson";
    ptr->daughter = "Marla Anderson";
    output(ptr);
```

```
}

// notice no class name
void output(family *ptr)
{
   cout << "husband is " << ptr->husband  << "\n"
        << "wife is " << ptr->wife  << "\n"
        << "son is " << ptr->son << "\n"
        << "daughter is " << ptr->daughter << "\n";
}
```

In the declaration of the class called family, we find that output() is declared as a friend function. This means that it is not a member function of the class family. However, it can access its private members husband, wife, son, daughter, and ptr since it is a friend. The output for this program follows:

```
husband is John Anderson
wife is Mary Anderson
son is Joey Anderson
daughter is Marla Anderson
```

■ **Friend functions are not affected by access specifiers.**

If the declaration of output() within class family is moved as follows:

```
class family
   {
   // private members follow
   private:
   char *husband[25];
   char *wife[25];
   char *son[25];
   char *daughter[25];
   // friend function inside private list
   friend void output(family *ptr);

   family *ptr;

   // public members follow
   public:
   void initialize(void);
   };
```

it would not mean that the friend function is private. That's the whole point of friend functions. They are *outside* functions that can access private and protected members of the class that they are friends of. Also, their function prototype need not necessarily exist. We included it to illustrate that no error messages would be generated during compilation, as they would have if it were a class member.

■ **All members of one class can become friends of another class via a single statement.**

Take a look at the following program that illustrates this concept.

```cpp
//     test12_12.cpp

#include <iostream.h>

// ** notice incomplete class declaration
class neighbor;

class family
    {
    // all functions of class neighbor are friends of
    // class family.
    friend neighbor;
    char *husband;
    char *wife;
    family *ptr;

    // public members follow
    public:
    void initialize(void);
    };

// Anderson is object of type family
family Anderson;

class neighbor
    {
    public:
    void output(family *ptr);
    };

// Davis is object of type neighbor
neighbor Davis;
main (void)
{
    Anderson.initialize();
}

void family::initialize(void)
{
    Anderson.ptr = &Anderson;
    ptr->husband = "John Anderson";
    ptr->wife    = "Mary Anderson";

    // send ptr to freind function output()
    Davis.output(Anderson.ptr);
}

void neighbor::output(family *ptr)
{
```

```
cout << "husband is " << ptr->husband << " \n"
     << "wife is " << ptr->wife     << " \n";
}
```

Compiling and running this program give the desired result:

```
husband is John Anderson
wife is Mary Anderson
```

Notice the incomplete declaration of class neighbor. It was necessary to do so, since reference is made to the class neighbor before it is declared. Remember, also, that objects of type neighbor cannot be declared unless the class declaration for neighbor is complete.

The function output() is declared as a member function of class neighbor. The class neighbor is declared a friend of the class family. Hence, all functions of the class neighbor become friends of the class family, even without this keyword having to prefix their individual declarations. This is why the friend function output() is able to access the private member ptr of family.

12.9 Inline Functions

There is one more subject to be discussed before this chapter is concluded, and that is the inline function. Inline functions provide a method for reducing function call overhead.

A member function can be defined within a class declaration, as is illustrated in the following example:

```
//    test12_13.cpp

#include <iostream.h>

class display
    {
    int i;
    public:

    // output() is an inline function
    void output(void)
        { cout << "i is " << i << "\n"; }

    };

// object_1 is an object of type display
display object_1;

main(void)
{
```

```
    object_1.output();
}
```

Compiling and executing this program give the following output:

```
i is 0
```

In the class declaration of display, the function output() is defined within the class itself. This is an example of an implicit inline definition.

- **Inline function declarations are defined within the class that they are declared in. They reduce function call overhead.**

Because the code of an inline function will become a part of each instance of that class, small functions are best suited to be inline within class declarations.

- **Inline functions can also be declared explicitly.**

Following is an example of an explicit declaration:

```
//    test12_14.cpp
#include <iostream.h>
class display
    {
    int i;
    public:

    // output() is defined inline elsewhere
    void output(void);
    };
// object_1 is an object of type display
display object_1;

// display is defined inline explicitly
inline void display::output(void)
{
    cout << "i is " << i << " \n";
}

main(void)
{
    object_1.output();
}
```

Executing this program gives the following output:

i is 0

The explicit declaration of the inline function output() is outside the class declaration, and is preceded by the keyword inline. This results in inline expansion of the code for the function output() each time this function is called.

■ **Inline functions must be defined before they can be referenced.**

Our program would not have compiled properly if the definition for output() existed below main().

12.10 REVIEW

In this chapter, features specific to class member declarations and definitions were described.

■ Class names must be unique within their scope.

■ A class member list can comprise any valid C++ data type.

■ Static class members allow multiple objects of a class type to share a location in memory. This reduces the need for global variables.

■ Structure members are public by default.

■ Class members are private by default.

■ Class members can have public, private, and protected access.

■ Class member functions follow the same scope and access rules as regular class members.

■ friend functions have access to the private and protected members of a class.

■ inline functions reduce function call overhead. Small functions are best declared inline within a class.

Derived Classes

13.1 INTRODUCTION

When a child is born, he or she inherits certain characterisitics from the mother and some from the father. With the passage of time, this child develops traits which uniquely identify him or her. This child is a combination of characteristics inherited from the parents and those derived from the environment in which he or she lives.

As we grow older, our outlook on life changes. Our dreams, goals, and ambitions are derived from what we are taught and what we experience in the circle in which we grow and interact.

And then we pass on what we have learned and achieved to those who are near and dear to us, and give them the opportunity to build on what we built ourselves.

If you think of your life in a nutshell, you will realize just how much of it has been derived from what you inherited from your parents, what you learned in school, what you learned from the social structure, and what your own ambition drives you to achieve. If features inherited from your parents could be grouped together as one class, features learned in school as another, and features derived from your social structure as another, then you are analogous to a *derived* class, since you have inherited features from your *base* classes (your parents, education, and social strucuture), and you have added a few unique characteristics of your own (your ambitions, achievements, and more!). Derived classes, as they exist in C++, are analogous to the simple life story presented above. A derived class *inherits* characteristics from one or more base classes. Then, it adds a few unique features of its own. This class can then be used as a base class for some other derived class, and so on.

This is also how a *hierarchy* of classes is created. This is how one object is built from another. This is what makes C++ the powerful language that it is.

13.2 A SIMPLE C++ APPLICATION

A simple C++ application will be developed using the traditional structured program design approach. This application will add, find, modify, and delete records from a file. The code for the individual functions that will perform these tasks is not important. Therefore, it will suffice to simply output a statement indicating which function is being executed at the time. Here's the code:

```
/* test13_1.cpp */

#include <stdio.h>

/* function prototypes follow */
void add(void);
void find(void);
void modify(void);
void remove(void);

main()
{
   char string[2], option = '\0';

   while (option != 'q')
   {
   cout << "Please enter option: \n";
   cout << "<a>dd, <f>ind, <m>odify, <d>elete or <q>uit:";
   cin >> string;

   switch(option)
       {       /* start switch */
     case 'a':
       add();
       break;
     case 'f':
       find();
       break;
     case 'm':
       modify();
       break;
     case 'd':
       remove();
       break;
     case 'q':
       exit();
```

```
    default:
        printf ("Invalid input! Please re-enter. \n");
    }  /* end switch */

}  /* end while() */

    return (0);
}  /* end main() */

void add(void)
{
    cout << "Inside add() \n";
}

void find(void)
{
    cout << "Inside find() \n";
}

void modify(void)
{
    cout << "Inside modify() \n";
}

void delete(void)
{
    cout << "Inside delete() \n";
}
```

Compiling and running this program will result in the following message being output on the screen:

```
Please enter option
<a>dd, <f>ind, <m>odify, <d>elete or <q>uit
```

On entry of a valid option, the corresponding function is executed. Otherwise, the message `Invalid option! Please re-enter` is displayed. Now we bring a small company into the picture. This company provides consulting services to its clients. Customer information is stored inside a master file.

Mr. Edward Heath is the owner of this company. He has four employees: Mary, Joseph, Ronald, and Sandra. Mr. Heath is interested in classifying the functions that can be performed by his employees. All of them should have the ability to find records from the master file. Only Mary and Joseph are allowed to add and modify records. Only he is allowed to delete them.

This logic can be incorporated inside the C++ program by assigning passwords to each employee. Access to various functions is allowed only on entry of a valid password. Mary and Joseph are assigned the passwords 10 and 20. Mr. Heath is assigned the password 99. Now take a look at the modified program.

```cpp
// test13_2.cpp

#include <stdio.h>

/* stdlib.h is required for atoi() */
#include <stdlib.h>

/* function prototypes follow */
void add(void);
void find(void);
void modify(void);
void remove(void);

main()
{
    char string[2], option = '\0';
    int i, *intptr;
    char *password, *charptr;

    cout << "Please enter password: ";

    // get input from user
    cin >> charptr;

    // convert to integer
    i = atoi(charptr);

    while (option != 'q')
    {
    cout << "Please enter option: \n";
    cout << "<a>dd, <f>ind, <m>odify, <d>elete or <q>uit:";

    // get option from user
    cin >> option;

    // switch on option entered
    switch(option)
        {
        case 'a':
          /* add() can be accessed by select employees */
              if (i == 10 || i == 11 || i == 99)
              add();
          else
              cout << "Permission denied!\n";
          break;

        // find() is accessible by all
        case 'f':
          find();
          break;

        // modify() is accessible by select employees
```

```
      case 'm':
          if (i == 10  || i == 20 || i == 99)
              modify();
          else
              cout << "Permission denied! \n";
          break;

        // delete is accessible by 1 person only
      case 'd':
          if (i == 99)
              remove();
          else
              cout << "Permission denied! \n";
          break;

      case 'q':
          exit();

      default:
          cout << "Invalid input! Please re-enter. \n";

      }  /* end switch */

  }  /* end while() */

  return (0);
}  /* end main() */

void add(void)
{
    cout << "Inside add() \n";
}

void find(void)
{
    cout << "Inside find() \n";
}

void modify(void)
{
    cout << "Inside modify() \n";
}

void remove(void)
{
    cout << "Inside delete() \n";
}
```

Notice that the header file <stdlib.h> is included. This header file contains the definition of the function atoi(), which simply converts an ASCII string to an integer. In the example, input for the password has to be converted to an integer to perform the correct checking. Based on the password entered, code is added inside the switch-case construct to restrict access to various functions.

Now let's rewrite this program using classes. The functions that can be performed by various employees will be grouped together into classes. The program will be broken up into its logical fragments, and each fragment will be explained before proceeding to the next. First, take a look at the class declarations:

```
// test13_1.cpp
// iostream.h is necessary for I/O
// stdio.h is necessary for getch()
// stdlib.h is necessary for atoi()
#include <iostream.h>
#include <stdio.h>
#include <stdlib.h>

class group_1
    {
    public:
    void find(void);
    };

// everyone is object of type group_1
group_1 everyone;

class group_2
    {
    public:
    void add(void);
    void modify(void);
    };

// select_few is object of type group_2
group_2 select_few;

class group_3
    {
    public:
    void add(void);
    void modify(void);

    // notice function name remove()
    // delete is a reserved word in C++
    void remove(void);
    };

// heath is object of type group_3
group_3 heath;
```

Three classes are declared. These are group_1, group_2, and group_3. Notice that group_2 and group_3 have two sets of functions that are exactly the same in name. These functions are add() and modify(). It is necessary for us to do this since we are interested in grouping together the set of functions that can be performed by one group as a separate entity. C++ allows us to do this through the use of classes.

Here's the main processing loop:

```
main(void)
{
     char string[2], option = '\0';
     int i, *intptr;
     char *password, *charptr;

     cout << "Please enter password: ";

   // get input from user
   // convert to integer
     charptr = gets(password);
     i = atoi(charptr);

     while (option != 'q')
     {    /* begin while() */

     cout << "Please enter option \n"
          << "<a>dd, <f>ind, <m>odify, <d>elete or <q>uit: ";

     cin  >> option;

     switch(option)
          {    // switch on option entered

          // select employees can access add()
          case 'a':
          if (i == 10 || i == 20)
          {
          select_few.add();
          }
          else if (i == 99)
          {
          heath.add();
          }
          else
          cout << "Permission denied \n";
          break;

     // everyone can access find()
     case 'f':
          everyone.find();
          break;

     // select few can access modify()

     case 'm':
          if (i == 10 || i == 20)
          {
          select_few.modify();
          }
```

```
                  else if (i == 99)
                  {
                  heath.modify();
                  }
                  else
                  cout << "Permission denied!";
                  break;

              // only heath can access remove()
            case 'd':
                  if (i == 99)
                  {
                  heath.remove();
                  }
                  else
                  cout << "Permission denied! \n";
                  break;

            case 'q':
             break;

            default:
                  cout << "Invalid option entered! \n";

        }     /* end switch */

        }     /* end while() */

    }     /* end main() */
```

In main(), the inherent logic is the same as in test13_2.cpp. However, we invoke member functions of different classes, based on the password entered, instead of the same copy of the appropriate function as we did in the prior programs. Take a look at the function definitions next:

```
//    function definitions follow

void group_1::find(void)
{
    cout << "Inside group1 find() \n";
}

void group_2::add(void)
{
    cout << "Inside group2 add() \n";
}

void group_2::modify(void)
{
    cout << "Inside group3 modify() \n";
}
```

```
// function definition of add() in group_3 follows
void group_3::add(void)
{
      cout << "Inside group3 add() \n";
}

// function definition of modify() in group_3 follows
void group_3::modify(void)
{
      cout << "Inside group3 modify() \n";
}

void group_3::remove(void)
{
      cout << "Inside group3 remove() \n";
}
```

Notice that there are two versions of add() and modify(), which are member functions of classes group_2 and group_3, respectively. There is only one version of remove(), which is a member function of class group_3. The output statement has been modified, in order to qualify exactly which function is being executed at any time.

Now if you look at the code for each version of these functions, you will realize that it is exactly the same. So how can multiple versions of the same code be eliminated, without the loss of the reasons for having them grouped together in the same class? The answer is through the use of derived classes.

13.3 DERIVED CLASSES IN C++

■ **C++ allows you to derive a class from one or more base classes. *A derived class inherits all members of its base class.***

■ **Access privileges of inherited members can be changed by the derived class through access specifiers that prefix the declaration of the base class.**

■ **Valid access specifiers are** public **and** private**.**

Take a look at this fragment of code:

```
class group_1
    {
    public:
    void find(void);
    };
// everyone is an object of type group_1
group_1 everyone;
```

This is a declaration of a base class. There is nothing unusual here. Now let's derive the class group_2 from it:

```
// notice declaration of class group_2
class group_2:public group_1
    {
    }
    // notice missing declaration of find()
    public:
    void add(void);
    void modify(void);
    };

// select_few is an object oftype group_2
group_2 select_few;
```

Now it's time to understand what happened.

The class group_2 is derived from the class group_1 via the statement:

```
class group_2:public group_1
```

The name of the first class in the list is that of the derived class. The name of the class following the colon (:) is that of the base class. The class group_2 inherits all members of its base class group_1. These members now belong to the member list of the class group_2. However, only the public and protected members of the base class can be used. (Protected members will be discussed in detail in the next chapter). The private members of the base class are not accessible to the derived class.

The access specifier public, which precedes the name of the base class, is used to specify access privileges of the inherited member list as they relate to the derived class:

```
class group_2:public group_1
```

This keyword indicates that the public members of the base class will also be public members inside the derived class. Along the same lines, protected members of the base class will be protected members inside the derived class. In other words,

■ *The keyword* public *indicates that the access privileges of the inherited members in the derived class will be the same as they exist in the base class.*

Remember, however, that

■ *The private members of the base class continue to remain private because they cannot be accessed by the derived class.*

This makes sense. The very idea behind private members of a class is to limit their access privileges. The whole point would be lost if derived classes were to inherit access to these members. A derived class is often used as a building block for some other object. If a hierarchy of ten derived classes were created and the private members of each class accessible to the next, then the advantages derived from the restriction of class members would be lost completely.

The following declaration of the derived class:

```
// ** notice keyword private
class group_2:private group_1
   {
   // notice missing declaration of find()
   public:
   void add(void);
   void modify(void);
   };

// select_few is an object of type group_2
group_2 select_few;
```

is synonymous to the following:

```
class group_2:group_1
   {
   public:
   void add(void);
   void modify(void);
   };
group_2 select_few;
```

This is because the default is private for a derived class. If this keyword prefixes the name of the base class, then both the public and protected members of the base class become private members of the derived class.

Now test13_1.cpp will be modified to use derived classes. The code will once again be presented in fragments, and each will be explained before proceeding to the next. First, the class declarations:

```
// test13_2.cpp

// iostream.h is necessary for I/O
// stdio.h is necessary for getch()
// stdlib.h is necessary for atoi()
#include <iostream.h>
#include <stdio.h>
#include <stdlib.h>

class group_1
   {
```

```
    public:
    void find(void);
    };

// everyone is an object of type group_1
group_1 everyone;

class group_2
    {
    public:
    void add(void);
    void modify(void);
    };

// select_few is an object of type group_2
group_2 select_few;

class group_3:public group_2
    {
    public:
    void remove(void);
    };

// heath is an object of type group_3
group_3 heath;
```

The class group_3 is derived from the class group_2. The base class group_2 is specified as public. This results in the functions add() and modify() also being public members for the class group_3. Now look at the code for main().

```
main(void)
{
    char string[2], option = '\0';
    int i, *intptr;
    char *password, *charptr;

    cout << "Please enter password: ";

    charptr = gets(password);
    i = atoi(charptr);

    while (option != 'q')
    {    /* begin while() */

    cout << "Please enter option \n"
        << "<a>dd, <f>ind, <m>odify, <d>elete or <q>uit: ";

    cin  >> option;

    switch(option)
            {    // start switch
```

```
        // select employees can access add()
        case 'a':
        if (i == 10 || i == 20)
        {
        select_few.add();
        }
        else if (i == 99)
        {
        heath.add();
        }
        else
        cout << "Permission denied \n";
        break;

    case 'f':
        everyone.find();
        break;

// select few can access modify()
    case 'm':
        if (i == 10 || i == 20)
        {
        select_few.modify();
        }
        else if (i == 99)
        {
        heath.modify();
        }
        else
        cout << "Permission denied!";
        break;

    case 'd':
        if (i == 99)
        {
        heath.remove();
        }
        else
        cout << "Permission denied! \n";
        break;

    case 'q':
     break;

    default:
        cout << "Invalid option entered! \n";

    }    /* end switch */

    }    /* end while() */

}    /* end main() */
```

The code is the same as test13_1.cpp. Now look at the function definitions:

```
//   function definitions follow
void group_1::find(void)
{
    cout << "Inside group1 find() \n";
}

void group_2::add(void)
{
    cout << "Inside group2 add() \n";
}

void group_2::modify(void)
{
    cout << "Inside group3 modify() \n";
}

void group_3::remove(void)
{
    cout << "Inside group3 remove() \n";
}
```

Notice that only one version of each function is defined. Compiling and running this program result in the following message being displayed on the screen:

```
Please enter password
```

Let's pretend that we are the designated empolyee of the month who has the privilege of deleting records from the master file (and the burden of living with the knowledge that a valid record might have been deleted!).

We enter the password 99. Let's enter option f to find a record. The following message is displayed on the screen:

```
Inside group1 find()
Please enter option
<a>dd  <f>ind  <m>odify  <d>elete, or <q>uit
```

Entering option a results in the following message being displayed:

```
Inside group2 add
Please enter option
<a>dd  <f>ind  <m>odify  <d>elete, or <q>uit
```

Entering d results in this message:

```
Inside group3 remove()
Please enter option
```

```
<a>dd  <f>ind  <m>odify  <d>elete, or <q>uit
```

and entering q allows exit from the program.

Now look at this fragment of code again:

```
case 'a':
        // select employees can access add()
    if (i == 10 || i == 20)
    {
    select_few.add();
    }
    else if (i == 99)
    {
    heath.add();
    }
```

As you can see, heath.add() is supposed to execute if the password is 99. However, there is no definition for heath.add()! The compiler accepted this because heath is an instance of the class group_3, and group_3 is derived from the class group_2. Hence, it inherits all public members of its base class.

■ **If functions are inherited by one class, then there is no need to redefine them.**

Refer to Figure 13.1 for a diagram of the logic implemented by the code.

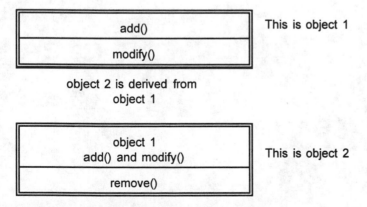

Figure 13.1 Creation of Objects

If the class group_2 can be considered an object, then the class group_3 contains that object, plus a unique function that differentiates it from group_2. group_3 cannot be group_3 without group_2. *Thus, one object is used as a building block for another.* The concept of derived classes should be clear to you now.

13.4 REVIEW

In this chapter, we learned the reasons for deriving a class from a base class, and how to do so. You should already understand the reason for using a class instead of a structure. Derived classes offer the advantages of classes in general, in addition to the ability to build a hierarchical structure of objects. The object at the top of the hierarchy is the most generalized object of the set. Each object derived from it contains features of the object from which it is derived, along with a few characteristics that make it unique.

You should now be thinking in terms of building objects, instead of writing procedural loops, as you were used to doing when you wrote code in C. The possiblities that can be gained from derived classes should now be emerging.

Access Privileges of Derived Classes

14.1 INTRODUCTION

In this chapter, access privileges of inherited members of classes derived from public and private base classes will be explained. But first, here's a discussion on protected members.

14.2 PROTECTED MEMBERS IN A CLASS

Consider the following class declaration:

```
class group_1
    {
    int a;   // a is private by default;
    protected:
    int b;   // b is protected
    public:
    void output1(void);
    }
group_1 everyone;
```

group_1 is a class in which a is a private member, b is a protected member, and the function output1() is public. Now look at the complete program.

```cpp
//   test14_1.cpp

#include <iostream.h>

class group_1
    {
    // a is private by default
    int a;

    // b is protected
    protected:
    int b;

    // output() is public
    public:
    void output1(void);
    };
group_1 everyone;

// group_2 is derived from group_1
class group_2:public group_1
    {
    // c is private by default
    int c;

    public:
    void output2(void);
    };
group_2 a_few;

void main(void)
{
    everyone.output1();
}

void group_1::output1(void)
{
    a = 5;
    b = 10;
    cout << "a is " << a << " b is " << b << "\n";
    a_few.output2();
}
void group_2::output2(void)
{
    c = 15;
    b += 10;
    cout << "c is " << c << " b is " << b << "\n";
}
```

Compiling and running this program will yield the following output:

```
a is 5 b is 10
c is 15 b is 20
```

Class members a and b are private and public members, respectively, of the class group_1. Hence, there are no suprises when the compiler allows access to these members from the function output1(), which is also a member function of that group. The protected member b is also accessed from this function and output2. output2 is a public member of the class group_2. Thus,

■ **Protected members of a base class are accessible by members of the derived class.**

Note here that group_2 is derived from group_1; that is, it inherits all members of group_1. Hence, the compiler does not issue any error messages when a class member of group_1 is accessed by a class member function of group_2 (if the class members of group_1 are either public or protected).

Let's modify the program and try to access the private member a from output2().

```cpp
//    test14_2.cpp

#include <iostream.h>

class group_1
    {
    int a;
    protected:
    int b;
    public:
    void output1(void);
    };
group_1 everyone;

// group_2 is derived from group_1
class group_2:public group_1
    {
    int c;
    public:
    void output2(void);
    };
group_2 a_few;

void main(void)
{
    everyone.output1();
}

void group_1::output1(void)
{
    a = 5;
    b = 10;
    cout << "a is " << a << " b is " << b << "\n";
```

```
      a_few.output2();
}
void group_2::output2(void)
{
      c = 15;
      b += 10;

     // private member is accessed
      cout << "a is " << a << "\n";
      cout << "c is " << c << " b is " << b << "\n";
}
```

Compiling and running this program result in the following error message:

```
Error:   'group_1::a' is not accessible
```

This program illustrates that

■ **Private members of a base class are not accessible to members of the derived class.**

Recall that we stated this in the previous chapter. Note that no error message is generated when a is accessed inside group_1::output1().

Now let's modify this program one more time and see if private and protected members of a base class are accessible to the public at large. You should already know the answer to this one, but we will present the code to reinforce what you may already know.

```
//    test14_3.cpp

#include <iostream.h>

class group_1
      {
      int a;
      protected:
      int b;
      public:
      void output1(void);
      };
group_1 everyone;

// group_2 is derived from group_1
class group_2:public group_1
      {
      int c;
      public:
      void output2(void);
      };
```

```
group_2 a_few;

void main(void)
{
    cout << "a is " << a " b is " << b << "\n";
    everyone.output1();
}
void group_1::output1(void)
{
    a = 5;
    b = 10;
    cout << "a is " << a << " b is " << b << "\n";
    a_few.output2();
}

void group_2::output2(void)
{
    c = 15;
    b += 10;
    cout << "c is " << c << " b is " << b << "\n";
}
```

Compiling this program results in the following error messages:

```
Error: Undefined symbol 'a'
       Undefined symbol 'b'
```

It would be safe to conclude that

- **Private and protected members of a base class can be accessed only by members of that class, and protected members of a base class can be accessed by members of classes derived from the same base class.**

14.3 ACCESS PRIVILEGES OF PUBLICLY DERIVED CLASSES

The following short program illustrates the access rules of members of base classes in derived classes.

```
//    test14_4.cpp

#include <iostream.h>

class group_1
    {
    int a;
    protected:
    int b;
    public:
    void output1(void);
```

```
        };
group_1 class1;

// group_2 is derived from group_1
class group_2:public group_1
        {
        public:
        void output2(void);
        };
group_2 class2;

// group_3 is derived from group_2
class group_3:public group_2
        {
        public:
        void output3(void);
        };
group_3 class3;

void main(void)
{
        class1.output1();
        class2.output2();
        class3.output3();
}

void group_1::output1(void)
{
        a = 5;
        b = 10;
        cout << "a is " << a << " b is " << b << "\n";
}

void group_2::output2(void)
{
        cout << "a is " << a << " b is " << b << "\n";
}

void group_3::output3(void)
{
        cout << "a is " << a << " b is " << b << "\n";
}
```

Compiling this program results in the following error messages:

```
Error: group_1::a is not accessible
       group_1::a is not accessible
```

Notice that no error messages were issued for accessing b, a protected member, from either one of the member functions of the derived classes group_2 or group_3. In conclusion, we can say that:

- **Public members of a base class continue to remain public for the derived class, and therefore, accessible to the public at large.**

The functions output2() and output3() were declared as public members of the derived classes group_2 and group_3. Hence, they could be called from main().

- **Protected members of a base class continue to remain protected for the derived classes.**

b is a protected member inside the base class group_1. Yet the compiler does not issue any error messages for this variable when it is accessed from member functions of the derived classes. The compiler would issue an error message if an attempt was made to access this variable from a nonmember function.

- **Private members of a base class continue to remain private to the base class. They cannot be accessed by member functions of derived classes.**

14.4 ACCESS PRIVILEGES OF PRIVATELY DERIVED CLASSES

Test14_4.cpp will now be modified to prefix the base class with the keyword private instead of public. Here's the code.

```
//    test14_5.cpp

#include <iostream.h>

class group_1
     {
     int a;
     protected:
     int b;
     public:
     void output1(void);
     };
group_1 class1;

// ** notice private declaration
class group_2:private group_1
     {
     public:
     void output2(void);
     };
group_2 class2;

// ** notice private declaration
```

```
class group_3:private group_2
         {
         public:
         void output3(void);
         };
group_3 class3;

void main(void)
{
     class1.output1();
     class2.output2();
     class3.output3();
}


void group_1::output1(void)
{
     a = 5;
     b = 10;
     cout << "a is " << a << " b is " << b << "\n";
}
void group_2::output2(void)
{
     cout << "a is " << a << " b is " << b << "\n";
}
void group_3::output3(void)
{
     cout << " b is " << b << "\n";
}
```

Compiling this program results in the following set of rather interesting error messages:

```
Error:   group_1::a is not accessible
         group_1::a is not accessible
         group_1::b is not accessible
         group_1::b is not accessible
```

Take a moment to analyze these error messages.

The first one states that group_1::a is not accessible in function group_2::output2(). This is understandable. a is a private member of the class group_1, and continues to remain private to its class. It cannot be accessed by members of derived classes.

The second message states that group_1::a is not accessible in the function group_3::output3(). This makes sense for the same reason as the first error message.

The third message states that group_1::b is not accessible in function group_3::output3(). This one should have gotten you thinking a bit. The reason this message was generated is because b is a protected member inside its base class. group_2 is privately derived from group_1.

The reason for this is

■ **Private derivation results in protected members of the base class becoming private members inside the derived class.**

Hence, b is now a private member for the derived class group_2. Therefore, b is inaccessible from a member function of group_3, since it is private for its base class, which is group_2. So why didn't we get this message when b was accessed from group_2::output2()? The reason is because b is a protected member inside group_1, and therefore accessible by members of the derived class group_2. However, since group_2 is privately derived, b becomes a private member for group_2, and therefore inaccessible to any subsequent derived classes.

Now that you understand the rules for access of private base members inside privately derived classes, let's modify test14_5.cpp and see how access privileges of public base members are affected by private derivation.

```
//    test14_6.cpp
#include <iostream.h>

class group_1
    {
    int a;
    protected:
    int b;
    public:
    void output1(void);
    };
group_1 class1;

// group_2 is privately derived
class group_2:private group_1
    {
    public:
    void output2(void);
    };
group_2 class2;

// group_3 is privately derived
class group_3:private group_2
    {
    public:
    void output3(void);
    };
group_3 class3;

void main(void)
{
    class1.output1();
```

```
        class2.output2();
        class3.output3();

        // public member output1() is accessed
        class2.output1();
        class3.output1();
}

void group_1::output1(void)
{
        a = 5;
        b = 10;
        cout << "a is " << a << " b is " << b << "\n";
}
void group_2::output2(void)
{
        cout << "a is " << a << " b is " << b << "\n";
}
void group_3::output3(void)
{
        cout << "a is " << a << " b is " << b << "\n";
}
```

Compiling this program results in the set of three error messages that the compiler issued in the previous program, in addition to these two:

```
Error: group_1::output1() is not accessible
       group_1::output1() is not accessible
```

These messages are generated for the following statements:

```
        class2.output1();
        class3.output1();
```

The reason for these messages is

■ **Public members of privately derived classes become private for the derived class.**

output1() is a public member of the class group_1. group_2 is privately derived from group_1. Hence, output1() becomes a private member of group_2. class2 is an instance of the class group_2. The statement class2.output1() is invoked from main(). But since output1() is now a private member of group_2, it can be accessed only by its class member list, and main() does not fall inside that category. This problem could be fixed by invoking class2.output1() inside the function group_2::output2() instead of main(), for example:

```
void group_2::output2(void)
{
    class2.output1();
```

```
    cout << "a is " << a << " b is " << b << "\n";
}
```

However, the following code would still present a problem:

```
void group_3::output3(void)
{
    class3.output1();
    cout << "a is " << a << " b is " << b << "\n";
}
```

The first invocation would be acceptable, since output1() is being accessed from output2(), which is a member function of the class group_2, and group_2 is derived from group_1. The second invocation would be unacceptable, since group_2 is privately derived from group_1; hence the public member output1() becomes private to group_1, and therefore inaccessible to group_3. Following is a complete program that would work. Code for the output of the variables a and b inside output2() and output3() have been taken out, as they are not applicable to what is being currently explained.

```
// test14_7.cpp

#include <iostream.h>

class group_1
    {
    int .a;
    protected:
    int b;
    public:
    void output1(void);
    };
group_1 class1;

//* notice private specifier for group_1 and group_2
class group_2:private group_1
    {
    public:
    void output2(void);
    };
group_2 class2;

class group_3:private group_2
    {
    public:
    void output3(void);
    };
group_3 class3;

void main(void)
{
    class1.output1();
```

```
        class2.output2();
        class3.output3();
}

void group_1::output1(void)
{
        a = 5;
        b = 10;
        cout << "a is " << a << " b is " << b << "\n";
}

void group_2::output2(void)
{
        // * output1 is accessed from output2()
        cout << "Inside output2() \n";
        class2.output1();
}

void group_3::output3(void)
{
        cout << "Inside output3() \n";
}
```

Another solution would have been simply to derive group_2 and group_3 publicly instead of privately. Which alternative you choose depends on how you want the visibility of these variables and functions to be affected.

The important point to note here is that

- *Data hiding*, **such as can be achieved via access specifiers for class member lists and base classes, is the key to designing** *modular* **programs.**

Your program should be composed of stand-alone sections that are easily identifiable, and therefore that much more flexible and modifiable. You can achieve this if you understand the scope of each variable, based upon the use of access specifiers. What is required is that you take the time to plan a hierachy of classes, determine access privileges for members of base classes inside derived classes, and understand exactly why you did what you did!

14.5 REVIEW

In this chapter, we described access privileges of base class members inside derived classes. Table 9.1 summarizes the major concepts with regard to access privileges.

Table 14.1 Access Privileges of Base and Derived Classes

Base Class Specifier	Access Inside Base Class	Access Inside Derived Class
public	Public Private Protected	Public Nonaccessible Protected
private	Public Private Protected	Private Nonaccessible Private

Constructors and Destructors

15.1 INTRODUCTION

In this chapter, we will discuss how C++ offers a mechanism for initializing classes when they are created and a corresponding mechanism for destroying them when they are no longer in scope, that is, no longer needed.

- **C++ allows automatic initialization of objects when they are created through *constructors*.**

- ***Destructors* are the opposite of constructors. They provide a way to deallocate memory that may have been allocated to objects through constructors.**

Before we begin our discussion on constructors and destructors, we want you to understand that the functionality that is available for constructors and destructors is called automatically if it is not invoked explicitly. The reason for explicitly calling constructors or destructors is to allocate or deallocate memory in those instances when the compiler does not operate as expected. For example, if a class object is not created properly, it may be necessary to deallocate memory originally allocated to it, and then to recreate it in a different location in memory. The reasons should become clearer to you as you read the remainder of this chapter.

The discussion will begin with constructors.

15.2 AN INTRODUCTION TO CONSTRUCTORS

Consider the following sample program:

```cpp
// test15_1.cpp

#include <iostream.h>

class sum
    {
    public:
    int sum_1;
    int sum_2;
    };
sum object_1, object_2;

void main(void)
{
    cout << "Inside main() \n";
    cout << "object_1.sum_1 is "<< object_1.sum_1 << "\n";
    cout << "object_1.sum_2 is "<< object_1.sum_2 << "\n";
    cout << "object_2.sum_1 is "<< object_2.sum_1 << "\n";
    cout << "object_2.sum_2 is "<< object_2.sum_2 << "\n";
}
```

Compiling and executing this simple program will result in the following output:

```
Inside main()
object_1.sum_1 is 0
object_1.sum_2 is 0
object_2.sum_1 is 0
object_2.sum_2 is 0
```

sum_1 and sum_2 are automatically initialized to zeros, since they are declared outside of main(), and never set to any other value. But suppose these class members were to contain some other values. Let's try to initialize these members inside the class declaration:

```cpp
// test15_2.cpp

#include <iostream.h>

class sum
    {
    // ** We try to initialize class members
    public:
    int sum_1 = 1;
    int sum_2 = 2;
    };
sum object_1, object_2;
```

```
void main(void)
{
   cout << "Inside main() \n";
   cout << "object_1.sum_1 is "<< object_1.sum_1 << "\n";
   cout << "object_1.sum_2 is "<< object_1.sum_2 << "\n";
   cout << "object_2.sum_1 is "<< object_2.sum_1 << "\n";
   cout << "object_2.sum_2 is "<< object_2.sum_2 << "\n";
}
```

Compiling this program will result in the following error message:

```
Error:  Cannot initialize a class member here
```

Therefore,

- **Class members cannot be initialized at the time that they are declared. Instead, C++ allows objects to be initialized at the time that they are created through constructors.**

15.3 DEFAULT CONSTRUCTORS

- **A constructor is a function that has the same name as the class that it initializes.**

- **Constructors can be defined inline, or outside the class declaration.**

- **Like ordinary function prototypes and definitions, constructors have no return value, and are called automatically by the compiler if they are not called explicitly.**

Take a look at test15_3.cpp:

```
// test15_3.cpp

 #include <iostream.h>

// function sum() has same name as class sum()
class sum
   {
   public:
   int sum_1;
   int sum_2;
   sum();
   };
sum object_1, object_2;
```

```
void main(void)
{
    cout << "Inside main() \n";

    cout << "object_1.sum_1 is "<< object_1.sum_1 << "\n";
    cout << "object_1.sum_2 is "<< object_1.sum_2 << "\n";
    cout << "object_2.sum_1 is "<< object_2.sum_1 << "\n";
    cout << "object_2.sum_2 is "<< object_2.sum_2 << "\n";
}

// sum::sum() is the constructor function

sum::sum()
{
    cout << "Inside sum() \n";
}
```

Compiling and executing this program will result in the following output:

```
Inside sum()
Inside sum()
Inside main()
object_1.sum_1 is 0
object_1.sum_2 is 0
object_2.sum_1 is 0
object_2.sum_2 is 0
```

As you look at the declaration of the class sum, you see that it has a class member also called sum(). This is a default constructor, and it is called as such because it has no arguments. (Constructors with arguments will be discussed later on in the chapter.) It is important to note that

■ **Constructors have the same name as the class in which they exist, they have no return type.**

The output of this program demonstrates an interesting feature about constructors. You were perhaps suprised to see that the print statement Inside sum() output before Inside main(). The reason for this is that the sum() constructor is called at the time that objects of type sum are created. Saying it a little bit differently,

■ **Constructors for objects are called at the time that objects of that type are declared.**

If you take a look at the test15_3.cpp, you will see that object_1 and object_2 are created outside of main(). Therefore, Inside sum() is output before Inside main(). Also, Inside sum() outputs twice, since two objects of type sum are created. sum() would have been called three times if three objects of that type had been created, and so on.

Another interesting feature is:

- **A default constructor is called implicitly by the compiler each time an object is declared, if one is not specified inside the class declaration.**

Just think back to all the programs in the previous chapters. Default constructors were being generated each time an object was declared, and you never even knew it!

The value of sum_1 and sum_2 continues to be zero, because these class objects are declared outside main() and they are not set to anything else. Let's see what happens if object_1 and object_2 are declared inside main().

```cpp
// test15_4.cpp

#include <iostream.h>

// function sum() has same name as class sum
class sum
    {
    public:
    int sum_1;
    int sum_2;
    sum();
    };

void main(void)
{
    // object_1 and object_2 are declared inside main()

    cout << "Inside main() \n";

    sum object_1, object_2;

    cout << "object_1.sum_1 is "<< object_1.sum_1 << "\n";
    cout << "object_1.sum_2 is "<< object_1.sum_2 << "\n";
    cout << "object_2.sum_1 is "<< object_2.sum_1 << "\n";
    cout << "object_2.sum_2 is "<< object_2.sum_2 << "\n";
}

// sum::sum() is the constructor function
sum::sum()
{
    cout << "Inside sum() \n";
}
```

Compiling and executing this program will give us the following results:

```
Inside main()
Inside sum()
Inside sum()
object_1.sum_1 is 0
object_1.sum_2 is 8815
object_1.sum_1 is 1
object_1.sum_2 is 0
```

This time the class members display garbage values. This is because objects of type sum are being created inside main(), so they are not global in scope, and hence not initialized to zero. So how can class members be initialized to specific values? The answer is:

- **Class members can be initialized through the use of parameters, or default arguments.**

Parameters will be discussed next.

15.4 CONSTRUCTORS WITH PARAMETERS

Take a look at test15_5.cpp:

```
// test15_5.cpp

#include <iostream.h>

class sum
    {
      // sum_1 and sum_2 are now private
    int sum_1;
    int sum_2;
    public:

      // sum() has no return type & arguments
    sum(int i, int j);
    };

void main(void)
{
    // ** object_1 & object_2 are created with parameters
    sum object_1(10,20), object_2(20,30);

    cout << "Inside main() \n";
}

sum::sum(int i, int j)
{
    // ** notice initialization to parameters
    sum_1 = i;
    sum_2 = j;
```

```
    cout << "sum_1 is " << sum_1 <<
        " sum_2 is " << sum_2 << "\n";
}
```

sum_1 and sum_2 are declared as private, since we are interested in utilizing the data hiding features that are offered by C++. Next, the constructor sum() is declared with arguments:

```
    sum(int i, int j);
```

Inside main(), object_1 and object_2 are declared with values substitued for the arguments:

```
    sum object_1(10,20), object_2(20,30)
```

Inside sum(), the two private class members sum_1 and sum_2 are initialized to the corresponding arguments i and j:

```
    sum_1 = i;
    sum_2 = j;
```

Compiling and executing this program will give the following output:

```
sum_1 is 10 sum_2 is 20
sum_1 is 20 sum_2 is 30
Inside main()
```

A couple of warnings are also issued in this (and subsequent programs, stating that object_1 and object_2 are never used inside main(). But these warnings will be overlooked, since these programs are meant to demonstrate specific features that relate to constructors, and the code does just that.

Notice that the class members of each object are initialized in the same order in which they are declared. Class members sum_1 and sum_2 of object_1 are created first, then initialized to 10 and 20, respectively. Next, class members sum_1 and sum_2 of object_2 are created, then initialized to 20 and 30, respectively.

15.5 CONSTRUCTORS WITH DEFAULT ARGUMENTS

Class members can be initialized in a variety of ways.

- **Default arguments can be specified in the constructor declaration. Class members will be initialized to these default values, if no others are specified.**

The following program illustrates what has just been said:

```cpp
// test15_6.cpp

#include <iostream.h>

class sum
    {
    // ** notice sum_1 and sum_2 are now private
    int sum_1;
    int  sum_2;

    public:
    // ** notice default arguments
    sum(int i, int j = 5);
    };

// ** object_1 is created with only 1 argument
sum object_1(10), object_2(20,30);

void main(void)
{
    cout << "Inside main() \n";
}
sum::sum(int i, int j)
{
    sum_1 = i;
    sum_2 = j;
    cout << "sum_1 is " << sum_1 <<
        " sum_2 is " << sum_2 << "\n";
}
```

The output for this program is as follows:

```
sum_1 is 10 sum_2 is 5
sum_1 is 20 sum_2 is 30
Inside main()
```

The declaration of the constructor sum is:

```
sum(int i, int j = 5);
```

The second parameter is initialized to a default value. Now notice the way object_1 and object_2 are created:

```
sum object_1(10), object_2(20,30);
```

Class member sum_1 for object_1 is initialized to 10 and sum_2 defaults to 5. The values for class members sum_1 and sum_2 for object_2 are self-explanatory.

15.6 OVERLOADING CONSTRUCTORS

■ **Constructors can be overloaded. That is, a constructor can have the same name, but different data types for arguments.**

The correct constructor will be invoked by the compiler, based on the data type of its argument. Take a look at test15_7.cpp:

```
// test15_7.cpp

#include <iostream.h>

class sum
    {
    int sum_1;
    double sum_2;
    public:

    // notice function name is overloaded
    sum(int i);
    sum(double k);
    };

void main(void)
{
    // ** sum(int) is called
    // ** sum(double) is called
    sum object_1(10);
    sum object_2(10.5);

    cout << "Inside main() \n";
}

sum::sum(int i)
{
    sum_1 = i;
    cout << "Inside sum(int) \n";
}

sum::sum(double k)
{
    sum_2 = k;
    cout << "Inside sum(double) \n";
}
```

Compiling and executing this program will produce the following output:

```
Inside sum(int)
Inside sum(double)
Inside main()
```

When object_1 is declared, the constructor sum(int) is invoked, since the parameter 10 is of type int. When object_2 is declared, the constructor sum(double) is invoked.

15.7 ORDER OF CALLING CONSTRUCTORS

The following program demonstrates the order in which constructors are called when dealing with base and derived classes:

```
// test15_8.cpp

#include <iostream.h>

class one
    {
    public:
    one();
    };

// ** two is derived from one
class two : public one
    {
    int b;
    public:
    two(int j);
    };

main(void)
{
    one object_1();
    two object_2(20);
    cout << "Inside main() \n";
}

one::one()
{
    cout << "Inside one \n";
}

two::two(int j)
{
    b = j;
    cout << "Inside two  b is " << b << "\n";
}
```

The class two is derived from one. Inside main(), an object of type one is declared and then an object of type two. The constructor one is a default constructor, since it takes no arguments. The constructor two is passed an argument. Compiling and executing this program result in the following output:

```
Inside one
Inside two  b is 20
Inside main()
```

The order in which the constructors are called is self-explanatory. But what would happen if an object of the type of the derived class only is created, and an object for the base class is not? Take a look at test15_9.cpp:

```cpp
// test15_9.cpp

#include <iostream.h>

class one
    {
    public:
    one();
    };

// two is derived from one
class two : public one
    {
    int b;
    public:
    two(int j);
    };

main(void)
{
    // ** We do not create object of type base class first
    two object_2(20);
    cout << "Inside main() \n";
}

one::one()
{
    cout << "Inside one \n";
}


two::two(int j)
{
    b = j;
    cout << "Inside two  b is " << b << "\n";
}
```

Compiling and executing this program will produce the following output:

```
Inside one
Inside two  b is 20
Inside main()
```

As you can see, the base class constructor is still called. This is necessary (and makes sense). Since two is derived from one, one must be constructed first. (How can you derive something from an object that does not exist? The base object must be created first.)

- **The base class constructor is constructed first and then the derived class constructor.**

Now take a look at the following program, which illustrates the order of calling constructors from multiple base classes.

```cpp
// test15_10.cpp

#include <iostream.h>

class one
    {
    public:
    one();
    };

class three
    {
    public:
    three();
    };

// ** notice multiple base classes
class two : public one, public three
    {
    int b;
    public:
    two(int j);
    };

main(void)
{
    two object_2(20);
    cout << "Inside main() \n";
}

one::one()
{
    cout << "Inside one \n";
}

two::two(int j)
{
    b = j;
    cout << "Inside two  b is " << b << "\n";
}
```

```
three::three()
{
    cout << "Inside three \n";
}
```

Compiling and executing this program produce the following output:

```
Inside one
Inside three
Inside two  b is 20
Inside main()
```

As you can see, the base class constructors are called in the same order in which they are declared:

```
class two : public one, public three
```

15.8 BASE CLASS CONSTRUCTORS WITH PARAMETERS

So far, so good. But what happens if you wish to create an object of a derived class whose base class requires parameters? Look at the following code, and you will understand what we mean:

```
// test15_11.cpp

#include <iostream.h>

class one
    {
    int a;
    public:
    one(int i);
    };
// ** two is derived from one
class two : public one
    {
    int b;
    public:
    two(int j);
    };

main(void)
{
    two object_2(20);
    cout << "Inside main() \n";
}

one::one(int i)
{
    a = i;
```

```
    cout << "Inside one a is " << a << "\n";
}

two::two(int j) : one(j)
{
    b = j;
    cout << "Inside two  b is " << b << "\n";
}
```

As you can see, the constructor for the base class one requires a parameter:

```
    one(int i);
```

The object two is derived from one:

```
class two : public one
```

and an object of type two is created with the required parameter:

```
    two object_2(20);
```

Then, there is an interesting definition for the constructor for the derived class:

```
two::two(int j) : one(j)
{   .
    .
}
```

This is one of the ways in which parameters can be sent to the base class. The definition of the constructor of the derived class follows the usual syntax. However, it is appended with a colon (indicating derivation), the name of the base class, and the parameter list.
Compiling and executing this program result in the following output:

```
Inside one a is 20
Inside two  b is 20
Inside main()
```

The order of calling the constructors (base class, then derived class) remains the same.

■ **Parameters can be passed to base classes in a variety of other ways as well. You can place a constant in the parameter list.**

Take a look at this program:

```
// test15_12.cpp

#include <iostream.h>

class one
    {
    int a;
    public:
    one(int i);
    };

// ** two is derived from one
class two : public one
    {
    int b;
    public:
    two(int j);
    };

main(void)
{
    two object_2(20);
    cout << "Inside main() \n";
}

one::one(int i)
{
    a = i;
    cout << "Inside one a is " << a << "\n";
}
// ** notice constant argument for one()
two::two(int j) : one(10)
{
    b = j;
    cout << "Inside two  b is " << b << "\n";
}
```

As you can see in the definition of the constructor for two:

```
two::two(int j) : one(10)
```

a constant is being sent as a parameter to one. Compiling and executing this program result in the following output:

```
Inside one a is 10
Inside two b is 20
Inside main()
```

The output should be self-explanatory.

- **Global parameters can also be passed to the base class constructor.**

Take a look at test15_13.cpp:

```
// test15_13.cpp
#include <iostream.h>

class one
    {
    int a;
    public:
    one(int i);
    };

class two : public one
    {
    int b;
    public:
    two(int j);
    };

// ** notice external variable declaration
int k;

main(void)
{
    // ** external variable is initialized
    k = 5;

    two object_2(20);
    cout << "Inside main() \n";
}

one::one(int i)
{
    a = i;
    cout << "Inside one a is " << a << "\n";
}

two::two(int j) : one(k)
{
    b = j;
    cout << "Inside two  b is " << b << "\n";
}
```

k is declared as a global variable, outside of main(), and initialized inside main() to 5. Then, it is passed as a parameter to the base class constructor:

```
two::two(int j) : one(k)
```

Compiling and executing this program will result in the following output:

```
Inside one a is 5
Inside two b is 20
Inside main()
```

The output should be self-explanatory.

15.9 DESTRUCTORS

The complement of a constructor is a destructor.

- **Destructors are used to deactivate the storage allocated to classes when they are created.**

- **Destructors have the same names as constructors, except that they are preceded by a tilde (~).**

Take a look at the following simple program which illustrates the use of a constructor and destructor:

```
//     test15_14.cpp

#include <iostream.h>

class one
    {
    // ** one() is the constructor
    // ** ~one() is the destructor
    public:
    one();
    ~one();
    };

main(void)
{
    cout << "Inside main() \n";
    one object_1;
    cout << "Inside main() - after creating object_1 \n";
}

// ** this is the constructor function
one::one()
{
    cout << "Inside one \n";
}

// ** this is the destructor function
one::~one()
{
    cout << "Inside ~one \n";
}
```

There are two member functions for the class one: these are one() and ~one(). one() is the default constructor, and ~one() is the destructor. Compiling and executing this program give the following output:

```
Inside main()
Inside one
Inside main() - after creating object_1
Inside ~one
```

As you can see, the destructor ~one is called automatically upon exit from main(). Like a constructor, it would have been called even if it had not explicitly defined.

■ **Like a constructor, a destructor does not have a return type or value.**

■ **Unlike constructors, destructors accepts no parameters.**

■ **Destructors are called implicitly when a variable goes out of scope (as it did in the sample program).**

For local variables, this occurs when they are no longer within block scope. For global variables, this occurs upon termination of the program.

15.10 ORDER OF CALLING DESTRUCTORS

■ **Destructors are called in the exact opposite order as constructors.**

Take a look at the following program:

```
//    test15_15.cpp

#include <iostream.h>

class one
    {
    public:
    one();
    ~one();
    };

// ** two is derived from one
class two : public one
    {
    public:
    two();
    ~two();
    };
```

```
main(void)
{
    cout << "Inside main() \n";
    two object_1;
    cout << "Inside main() - after creating object_1 \n";
}

// ** this is the base class constructor
one::one()
{
    cout << "Inside one \n";
}

// ** this is the base class destructor
one::~one()
{
    cout << "Inside ~one \n";
}

// ** this is the derived class constructor
two::two()
{
    cout << "Inside two \n";
}

// ** this is the derived class constructor
two::~two()
{
    cout << "Inside ~two \n";
}
```

Here the class two is derived from one. Compiling and executing this program will result in the following output:

```
Inside main()
Inside one
Inside two
Inside main() - after creating object_1
Inside ~two
Inside ~one
```

Inside main(), an object of type two is created. However, two is derived from one. Therefore, one is constructed first, and then two. Next, the program is exited. Here we see that first the destructor for the derived class is called (~two) and then the destructor for the base class (~one).

■ **Destruction follows the opposite order of construction, as it logically should.**

15.11 Review

In this chapter, we learned a lot of interesting things about constructors and destructors.

- Constructors are functions that have the same names as their classes. They initialize objects when they are created.

- They are called automatically by the compiler, if they are not explicity called within the program, at the time when objects of their class types are declared.

- Default arguments can be supplied to constructors.

- Constructors can be overloaded because the correct version will be automatically invoked by the compiler.

- They are called in the logical order that is followed by base and derived classes; i.e., base class constructors will precede derived class constructors.

- Destructors are the complement of constructors. They have the same names as constructors, except they are preceded by a tilde (~).

- Destructors deallocate memory allocated to objects created through constructors.

- They are called automatically upon exit from `main()`, if they are not explicitly called.

- They accept no parameters.

- Destructors are called in the opposite order as constructors; i.e., derived class destructors are called before base class destructors.

Chapter 16

Virtual Functions
and Polymorphism

16.1 INTRODUCTION

You have come a long way since you first started reading Chapter 1 of this book (and it has been a fairly smooth journey, we hope). In that chapter, we introduced you to the concept of a virtual function. At the time, it is unlikely that you understood the full power of this feature of C++. In this chapter, this concept will be reintroduced and illustrated in detail. You will be introduced to words such as *polymorphism*, and expressions such as *early binding* and *run-time binding*. By the time you conclude this chapter, you will feel comfortable with these little catch words, which C++ programmers and books freely use, and realize that these concepts are really not as difficult to understand as you may have originally thought.

16.2 BACK TO POINTERS

Before we begin our discussion of virtual functions, here is a short refresher on pointers. This discussion is necessary, since it is through pointers to base and derived classes that run-time polymorphism is achieved in C++.

A pointer, as you already know, contains the location in memory of a data type. For example, if you declare an integer variable in your program:

```
int a;   // a is an integer data type
```

then, a pointer to this variable would be declared, as follows:

```
int *ptr;   // ptr is a pointer to an integer
```

Next, `ptr` would be set to the address or location in memory of `a`:

```
ptr = &a;   // ptr is set to the address of a
```

Once this is done, the contents of the variable `a` can be accessed indirectly through `ptr`. The following two statements result in the same output:

```
*ptr = 5;   // access contents of a through ptr, set a to 5
a = 5;      // access contents of a directly, set a to 5
```

The location in memory of `a` would be obtained by preceding `ptr` with the * operator. The following statement illustrates this:

```
cout << "At location " << ptr << "is stored " << *ptr
```

The statement above would result in the following output on your computer:

```
At location xxxxxx is stored 5
```

where xxxxxx is the address of `a`. The first invocation of `ptr` results in the address of `a` being output. The second invocation of `ptr` results in the output of the contents of what is stored at that address.

16.3 POINTERS TO CLASSES

- **C++ has pointers to characters, floats, doubles, arrays, and the like. There are pointers to structures, and, in C++, you also have pointers to classes.**

- **The syntax for accessing class members via pointers is the same.**

    Take a look at the following program:

```
// test16_1.cpp

#include <iostream.h>

class one
    {
    public:
```

```
    void output(void)
      {
      cout << "Inside output \n";
      }
    };
main(void)
{
    // object_1 is object of type one
    // pointer is pointer to object of type one
    one object_1;
    one *pointer;

    // pointer is set to address of object_1
    // output() is executed
    pointer = &object_1;
    pointer->output();

    return(0);
}
```

Compiling and executing this program will result in the following output:

```
Inside output
```

First, the class one is declared. The function output() is inline. (It is defined within the class.) Inside main(), object_1 as an object of type one. Then, pointer is declared as a pointer to objects of type one. pointer is set equal to the address of object_1. Next, the class member output() of the class one is executed via the statement:

```
pointer->output();
```

The -> operator is one way to access a class member through a pointer. The following statement would have given the same result:

```
pointer.output();
```

We will use the -> operator in our programs, since the arrow intuitively symbolizes that something is being pointed to, and that is exactly what is being implemented in the program.

16.4 POINTERS TO DERIVED CLASSES

■ **In C++, there exist pointers to base classes and pointers to derived classes.**

■ **Members of a derived class can be accessed via a pointer to the base class, as long as the member being accessed in the derived class has been inherited from the base class.**

This will become clear as you read the next program:

```
// test16_2.cpp

#include <iostream.h>

class one
    {
    public:
    void output(void)
        {
        cout << "Inside output \n";
        }
    };

// two is derived from one
class two : public one
    {
    public:
    void output2(void)
        {
        cout << "Inside output2 \n";
        }
    };

main(void)
{
    // object of type one is declared
    // object for derived class is declared
    // pointer to base class is declared
    one object_1;
    two object_2;
    one *pointer;

    // pointer is set to address of object_1
    // object_1::output() is executed
    pointer = &object_1;
    pointer->output();

    // pointer is now set to address of derived class
    // object_2::output() is executed
    pointer = &object_2;
    pointer->output();

    return(0);
}
```

Compiling and running this program will result in the following output:

```
Inside output
Inside output
```

Here is the original definition of class one. Then class two is publicly derived from one. The class one has one class member: output(), and the class two has two class members: output(), which it inherits from class one, and output2(), which is unique to it.

Inside main(), a pointer is declared to the base class one. Next, it is set to the address of object_1, which is an object of type one. The function output() is executed as follows:

```
pointer->output();
```

Next, pointer is set to the address of an object of type two, which is the derived class:

```
pointer = &object_two;
```

and output() is executed again:

```
pointer->output();
```

The compiler did not generate any errors since the function output() for object_two is inherited from the base class one. If test16_2.cpp is modified to execute output2() (which is a unique member function of two.) via the pointer to the base class, then errors will be encountered, as this program illustrates:

```
// test16_3.cpp

#include <iostream.h>

class one
    {
    public:
    void output(void)
        {
        cout << "Inside output \n";
        }
    };

// two is derived from one
class two : public one
    {
    public:
    void output2(void)
        {
        cout << "Inside output2 \n";
        }
    };
```

```
main(void)
{
    // object of type one is declared
    // object for derived class is declared
    // pointer to base class is declared
    one object_1;
    two object_2;
    one *pointer;

    // pointer is set to address of object_1
    // object_1::output() is executed
    pointer = &object_1;
    pointer->output();

    // pointer is now set to address of derived class
    // object_2::output2() is executed
    pointer = &object_2;
    pointer->output2();

    return(0);
}
```

Compiling and executing this program will result in the following message:

```
Error:   output2 is not a member of one
```

The compiler issued this complaint in response to the following statement:

```
pointer->output2();
```

This is because `pointer` is declared as a pointer to the base class `one`, and `output2()` is specific to the class `two`, not inherited from `one`.

Incidentally, you can typecast the base class pointer as a pointer to the derived class, and succeed in executing `output2` through pointer as follows:

```
((two *)pointer)->output2();
```

We don't want to get into too many messy details about statements that look like the one above (confusing, to say the least), and hence won't elaborate on it further in this chapter.

■ **Elements of the derived class that are not inherited from the base class can be accessed through a pointer to the derived class.**

Take a look at this version of the program:

```
// test16_4.cpp

#include <iostream.h>

class one
    {
    public:
    void output(void)
        {
        cout << "Inside output \n";
        }
    };
// two is derived from one
class two : public one
    {
    public:
    void output2(void)
        {
        cout << "Inside output2 \n";
        }
    };

main(void)
{
    // object of type one is declared
    // object for derived class is declared
    // pointer to base class is declared
    // pointer to derived class is declared
    one object_1;
    two object_2;
    one *pointer;
    two *pointer2;

    // pointer is set to address of object_1
    // object_1::output() is executed
    pointer = &object_1;
    pointer->output();

    // pointer is now set to address of derived class
    // object_2::output2() is executed
    pointer2 = &object_2;
    pointer2->output2();

    return(0);
}
```

Compiling and running this program will result in the following output:

```
Inside output
Inside output2
```

16.5 VIRTUAL FUNCTIONS REVISITED

With this introduction to pointers to base and derived classes, we return to our discussion on virtual functions. It is necessary for you to understand how class members are accessed through pointers, since this is the fundamental mechanism by which virtual functions are executed.

So exactly what does the word *polymorphism* mean? We refer to our handy *Webster's Encyclopedic Unabridged Dictionary*, and narrow in on the following explanations:

"...existence of an animal or plant in several form or color varieties..."

"...state or condition of being polymorphous..."

Meanwhile, polymorphous means

"...having, assuming, or passing through many or various forms..."

Think about the first definition for a minute. Think of a rose. A rose is a rose, but some roses are red, some are white, and some are pink, and maybe one day someone will somehow create a rose that is black or some other peculiar color.

Now think of a rose as an object. We know that a rose is a rose because it is of a certain shape, its petals are soft, it has a distinct bouquet, and it has thorns on its stems. Now we are not quite sure of how a rose came into existence, or who created it, but let's attribute its existence to nature. Nature created a flower of this specific shape, and gave it the remaining attributes that made it a rose. And when everything was ready, suppose it left the implementation of the color to a different entity. It would send a rose with no color, or a default color (say red), to the entity and allow it to determine the exact method in which a specific color would be assigned to that particular rose. This entity would determine the color of the rose in its own distinct way, and pass the color back to nature. Each time a new color had to be assigned to the rose, nature would send the default rose to the entity, and after the color was assigned, the rose would be sent back to nature.

The interface or interconnection is the same each time a rose is sent: a rose with no or default color. The object returned from the entity is also always the same: a rose with a color. However, the way the color is determined, or the method in which it is assigned, is different for each color. If a green rose were to be created, then the colors yellow and blue would have to be mixed. If a purple rose were to be created, then the colors red and blue would have to be mixed, and so on. There is only one interface, but there are multiple-implementations. Based on the definition from the dictionary, believe it or not, a rose is polymorphous because it can exist in several color varieties. Furthermore, believe it or not, this *one interface, multiple-implementations concept is the key to understanding polymorphism in C++.*

We will now build on the one interface, multiple-implementations concept, using a different example and sample programs, to help you further understand this powerful object-oriented mechanism.

We know of a little travel agency that specializes in Caribbean vacation packages. When this agency first started out, the owners decided to design a program in C++ that would list the salient attractions of the Caribbean resorts included in each package. The astute programmer who was assigned this task understood the advantages of using classes instead of structures, and so decided to build a class hierarchy where the base class would describe those features which are common to all Caribbean islands. Each island would then be derived from the base class and contain descriptions of the attractions that are specific to the island.

This program was designed to be as flexible as possible so that changes could be easily incorporated into it. What if a hurricane struck one island, or local tensions broke out in another? Obviously, these islands would have to be taken off the list of available packages. At the same time, new packages may be added as the company grows. What was needed was a program that could add and delete functions that were inherently the same (i.e., the listed attractions) but were implemented differently (a different set of attractions would be listed for each island). Based on these needs, it was apparent that virtual functions were the answer. Here's the result:

```
// test16_5.cpp

#include <iostream.h>

// caribbean_isles will be the main base class
class caribbean_isles
    {
    public:

    // ** notice keyword virtual
    virtual void other_attractions(void)
        {
        cout << "!!COME VISIT THE CARRIBBEAN ISLANDS!! \n";
        cout << "White sandy beaches \n";
        cout << "Crystal clear water \n";
        cout << "No hassles - No worries - No cares \n\n";
        }
    };
```

The code is broken up into logical fragments, since it is longer than most of the other programs in this book. The program starts off by declaring a base class called `caribbean_isles`. This class contains one public function called `other_attractions()`. The definition of this function is preceded by the keyword *virtual*. It is inline (it does not have to be), and it outputs those features which are common to all Caribbean Islands in the list of available packages: white sand beaches; crystal clear water; and no hassles, worries, or cares. Let's continue with the code:

```
// bahamas, grand_cayman and st_thomas are derived from
// caribbean_isles.
class bahamas : public caribbean_isles
    {
    public:

    // ** notice same function name, no keyword virtual
    void other_attractions(void)
        {
        cout << "!!BAHAMAS!! \n";
        cout << "Fun-filled casinos \n";
        cout << "Action-packed water sports \n";
        cout << "Great rum punches \n\n";
        }
    };

class grand_cayman : public caribbean_isles
    {
    public:

    // ** notice same function name, no keyword virtual
    void other_attractions(void)
        {
        cout << "!!GRAND CAYMAN!! \n";
        cout << "Incredible scuba diving \n";
        cout << "Big time game fishing \n";
        cout << "Duty free shopping \n\n";
        }
    };

class st_thomas : public caribbean_isles
    {
    public:

    // ** notice same function name, no keyword virtual
    void other_attractions(void)
        {
        cout << "!!ST THOMAS!! \n";
        cout << "Excellent shopping \n\n";
        }
    };
```

Next, the bahamas, grand_cayman, and st_thomas are derived from the caribbean_isles. These islands inherit all features contained in the caribbean_isles, and then add a few features of their own. Notice here that each of these classes contains a member function whose name is common to the virtual function in the base class (other_attractions()). In addition to this, the return type is the same (void), and so are the parameters (void again). However, the implementation of each function is different (a different set of attractions is listed for each method). Now take a look at the code for main():

```
main(void)
{
    // ** object and ptr to caribbean_isles class is declared
    caribbean_isles islands, *ptr;

    // objects for derived classes are declared
    bahamas package_1;
    grand_cayman package_2;
    st_thomas package_3;

    // ptr is set to address of base class object
    ptr = &islands;

    // virtual function is executed
    // the compiler will know which version to execute!!
    ptr->other_attractions();

    // ptr is now set to address of derived class objects
    ptr = &package_1;
    ptr->other_attractions();
    ptr = &package_2;
    ptr->other_attractions();
    ptr = &package_3;
    ptr->other_attractions();

    return(0);
}
```

Inside main(), objects of the base and derived classes and a pointer to the base class are declared. Next, ptr is set to the address of the base class, and the function other_attractions() is implemented. But which version of the function will be implemented? Well, C++ determines the answer to this question at *run* time, as opposed to *compile* time, based on the type of object that is being pointed to. This is called *late binding*, and *run-time polymorphism*. These little catch words should be starting to make sense now.

Compiling and executing this program will result in the following output:

!!COME VISIT THE CARRIBBEAN ISLANDS!!

```
White sandy beaches
Crystal clear water
No hassles - No worries - No cares

!!BAHAMAS!!
Fun-filled casinos
Action-packed water sports
Great rum punches

!!GRAND CAYMAN!!
Incredible scuba diving
Big time game fishing
Duty free shopping

!!ST THOMAS!!
Excellent shopping
```

Now let's understand the output.

Initially, ptr is set to point to the object islands, which is an instance of the class object of type caribbean_isles. Hence, the statement:

```
ptr->other_attractions();
```

results in the execution of the version of other_attractions() that belongs to the base class.

Next, ptr is set to point to the object package_1, which is an instance of type bahamas. Hence, the statement:

```
ptr->other_attractions();
```

results in the execution of the version of other_attractions() that belongs to the derived class bahamas.

Step through the remainder of the program yourself, and you should be able to understand which version is being implemented, and why.

16.6 WHAT IS A VIRTUAL FUNCTION?

- A *virtual function* is one that is declared as such in the base class. Then, it is redefined (although it does not have to be, as you will see shortly), in one or more classes derived from the base class.

- The correct implementation of the function is selected at run time, as opposed to compile time, based on the object that is being pointed to.

- A virtual function is preceded by the keyword *virtual* inside the base class. This function is redefined inside the derived classes.

■ **The name, return type, and parameters for the function must be exactly the same as those in the original prototype in the base class, otherwise the virtual nature of these functions is lost.**

For this reason, we do not use the term *overloaded* to describe these special functions. (Recall that overloaded functions have the same name, but different parameters.) Instead, the function is *overridden* inside the derived class.

■ **Run-time polymorphism is achieved by accessing these functions through a pointer to the base class.**

The base class specifies the functions that will be common to all classes derived from it. It provides the uniform interface to these functions inside the derived classes. The actual method in which this function will be implemented is defined inside the derived class.

16.7 WHAT ARE EARLY BINDING AND LATE BINDING?

■ *Early binding* **indicates the occurrence of the determination of events that are to take place at the time that a program is compiled.**

Examples of early binding are standard and overloaded function calls. Information required to implement standard and overloaded functions is known at the time that a program is compiled.

■ *Late binding* **indicates the occurrence of the determination of events that are to take place at the time that a program is run.**

Examples of late binding include virtual functions. Information required to implement virtual functions is known at the time that a program is run, not when it is compiled. Let's explain this a little bit further.

Take a look at this very simple program:

```
// test16_6.cpp

main(void)
{
    int a = 5;  // 1st statement
    a += 2;     // 2nd statement
}
```

Compiling and executing this program will generate no errors and produce no output; we have deliberately kept it this simple. However, this program illustrates two major points.

The first statement is executed at compile time. When test16_6.cpp is compiled, the compiler assigns storage for an integer to the variable a, and stores the value of 5 in it.

The second statement is executed at run time. When test16_6.cpp is run, 2 is added to whatever is stored in a.

So why are virtual functions a run-time phenomenon? Well, you already know that the function that is to execute is determined by the object being pointed to at the time. The value of ptr is modified at run time. Hence, the related version of the function that is to execute is also determined at run time.

16.8 REVIEW

In this chapter, we learned the how and why of virtual functions. We learned:

- How pointers to base and derived classes are used to invoke function class members.

- That a pointer to a base class can be used to access a member of the derived class, as long as that class member has been inherited from the base.

- How virtual functions can be invoked using pointers to base classes to access objects of different types. Terms such as *late binding* and *run-time polymorphism* are used to describe this phenomenon.

Virtual Functions and Abstract Classes

17.1 INTRODUCTION

In the previous chapter, we reintroduced virtual functions and explained how they are invoked and why. In this chapter, we will build on this concept further, and introduce you to pure virtual functions and abstract classes.

17.2 FLEXIBILITY OF VIRTUAL FUNCTIONS

In Chapter 15, a C++ program was designed that listed the main attractions of the vacation packages offered by our travel agency. This program was designed in such a way that it would be flexible enough to handle deletion and insertion of islands to the packages, without major redesign of the main code. This objective was achieved by utilizing virtual functions. It is presented in its entirety here for your convenience.

```
// test11_5.cpp

#include <iostream.h>

// caribbean_isles will be the main base class
class caribbean_isles
    {
    public:

    // ** notice keyword virtual
    virtual void other_attractions(void)
        {
```

```
      cout << "!!COME VISIT THE CARRIBBEAN ISLANDS!! \n";
      cout << "White sandy beaches \n";
      cout << "Crystal clear water \n";
      cout << "No hassles - No worries - No cares \n\n";
      }
};

// bahamas, grand_cayman and st_thomas are derived from
// caribbean_isles.

class bahamas : public caribbean_isles
   {
   public:

   // ** notice same function name, no keyword virtual
   void other_attractions(void)
      {
      cout << "!!BAHAMAS!! \n";
      cout << "Fun-filled casinos \n";
      cout << "Action-packed water sports \n";
      cout << "Great rum punches \n\n";
      }
};

class grand_cayman : public caribbean_isles
   {
   public:

   // ** notice same function name, no keyword virtual
   void other_attractions(void)
      {
      cout << "!!GRAND CAYMAN!! \n";
      cout << "Incredible scuba diving \n";
      cout << "Big time game fishing \n";
      cout << "Duty free shopping \n\n";
      }
};

class st_thomas : public caribbean_isles
   {
   public:

   // ** notice same function name, no keyword virtual
   void other_attractions(void)
      {
      cout << "!!ST THOMAS!! \n";
      cout << "Excellent shopping \n\n";
      }
};

main(void)
{
   // ** object and ptr to caribbean_isles class is declared
   caribbean_isles islands, *ptr;
```

```
// objects for derived classes are declared
bahamas package_1;
grand_cayman package_2;
st_thomas package_3;

// ptr is set to address of base class object
ptr = &islands;

// virtual function is executed
// the compiler will know which version to execute!!
ptr->other_attractions();

// ptr is now set to address of derived class objects
ptr = &package_1;
ptr->other_attractions();
ptr = &package_2;
ptr->other_attractions();
ptr = &package_3;
ptr->other_attractions();

return(0);
}
```

Now suppose a fourth hot-spot package comes into the picture. The
code of the original program would be modified as follows:

```
// test1_1.cpp

#include <iostream.h>

// caribbean_isles will be the main base class
class caribbean_isles
    {
    public:

    // ** notice keyword virtual
    virtual void other_attractions(void)
        {
        cout << "!!COME VISIT THE CARRIBBEAN ISLANDS!! \n";
        cout << "White sandy beaches \n";
        cout << "Crystal clear water \n";
        cout << "No hassles - No worries - No cares \n\n";
        }
    };

// bahamas, grand_cayman and st_thomas are derived from
// caribbean_isles.

class bahamas : public caribbean_isles
    {
    public:

    // ** notice same function name, no keyword virtual
```

```
    void other_attractions(void)
        {
        cout << "!!BAHAMAS!! \n";
        cout << "Fun-filled casinos \n";
        cout << "Action-packed water sports \n";
        cout << "Great rum punches \n\n";
        }
    };

class grand_cayman : public caribbean_isles
    {
    public:

    // ** notice same function name, no keyword virtual
    void other_attractions(void)
        {
        cout << "!!GRAND CAYMAN!! \n";
        cout << "Incredible scuba diving \n";
        cout << "Big time game fishing \n";
        cout << "Duty free shopping \n\n";
        }
    };

class st_thomas : public caribbean_isles
    {
    public:

    // ** notice same function name, no keyword virtual
    void other_attractions(void)
        {
        cout << "!!ST THOMAS!! \n";
        cout << "Excellent shopping \n\n";
        }
    };

class st_lucia : public caribbean_isles
    {
    public:

    // ** notice same function name, no keyword virtual
    void other_attractions(void)
        {
        cout << "!!ST LUCIA!! \n";
        }
    };

main(void)
{
    // ** object and ptr to caribbean_isles class is declared
    caribbean_isles islands, *ptr;
    // objects for derived classes are declared
    bahamas package_1;
    grand_cayman package_2;
    st_thomas package_3;
```

```
// ** st_lucia package is added here
st_lucia package_4;

// ptr is set to address of base class object
ptr = &islands;

// virtual function is executed
// the compiler will know which version to execute!!
ptr->other_attractions();

// ptr is now set to address of derived class objects
ptr = &package_1;
ptr->other_attractions();
ptr = &package_2;
ptr->other_attractions();
ptr = &package_3;
ptr->other_attractions();

// ** ptr to address of st_lucia is added here

ptr = &package_4;
ptr->other_attractions();

return(0);
}
```

As you can see, a new class st_lucia has been added. This is the latest hot-spot package which will contain its own implementation of other_attractions(). Now take a look at the code for main().

The following lines of code are the only changes required inside main() to implement the function for the new derived class:

```
st_lucia package_4;
```

and

```
ptr = &package_4;
ptr->other_attractions();
```

The output for this program is the same as that of test11_5.cpp, in the previous chapter, with one additiona line of output: !!ST LUCIA!!. This program illustrates the ease with which new functions can be integrated into the program. Removing the assignment of a pointer to a derived class would illustrate the corresponding ease with which virtual functions can be removed from the main logic.

17.3 DEVIATIONS FROM THE NORM

There is a small island in the heart of the Caribbean. Not many know about it, but this quaint little haunt has majestic mountains, white sandy beaches, and breathtaking undersea cliffs. This island's name is Saba.

Suppose this island was to be included as one of the prime attractions, called the *mystery package*. However, at the moment, no one is quite sure how to classify its attractions. So, how would this situation be handled? Well, we forgot to tell you.

- **If a virtual function is not defined inside the derived class, then the base virtual function is automatically executed instead.**

Or, to say it a different way, *if a derived class does not provide a function to override the base virtual function, then the base virtual function will execute when an object of the type of the new class is pointed to.* We will modify the original program to illustrate how this happens:

```cpp
// test17_2.cpp

#include <iostream.h>

// caribbean_isles is the main base class
class caribbean_isles
    {
    public:

    // ** we will output the header separately
    void header(void)
        { cout << "!!COME VISIT THE CARIBBEAN ISLANDS!! \n";}

    virtual void other_attractions(void)
        {
        cout << "White sandy beaches \n";
        cout << "Crystal clear water \n";
        cout << "No hassles - No worries - No cares \n\n";
        }
    };
```

As you can see, this is a modified definition of the base class. It was modified by outputting the header line separately from the remainder of the original function. The new header function is not declared as virtual, since there is no need to do so. Let's continue with the program.

```cpp
// bahamas, grand_cayman and st_thomas are derived from
// caribbean_isles.
// ** so is saba
class bahamas : public caribbean_isles
    {
    public:

    // ** notice same function name, no keyword virtual
    void other_attractions(void)
```

```
      {
      cout << "!!BAHAMAS!! \n";
      cout << "Fun-filled casinos \n";
      cout << "Action-packed water sports \n";
      cout << "Great rum punches \n\n";
      }
   };

class grand_cayman : public caribbean_isles
   {
   public:

   // ** notice same function name, no keyword virtual
   void other_attractions(void)
      {
      cout << "!!GRAND CAYMAN!! \n";
      cout << "Incredible scuba diving \n";
      cout << "Big time game fishing \n";
      cout << "Duty free shopping \n\n";
      }
   };

class st_thomas : public caribbean_isles
   {
   public:

   // ** notice same function name, no keyword virtual
   void other_attractions(void)
      {
      cout << "!!ST THOMAS!! \n";
      cout << "Excellent shopping \n\n";
      }
   };

class saba : public caribbean_isles
   {
   public:
   void name(void) { cout << "!!MYSTERY ISLAND SABA!! \n"; };

   // ** attributes of other_attractions() not defined yet

   };
```

The class saba is defined just as the rest. However, the attributes of its function other_attractions() have not been determined yet. These attributes are expected to be known some time in the future. For now, the mystery island simply inherits attributes from its base class. Let's continue with main().

```
main(void)
{
   // declare object and ptr to caribbean_isles class
   caribbean_isles islands, *ptr;
```

```
// declare objects for derived classes
bahamas package_1;
grand_cayman package_2;
st_thomas package_3;
saba mystery_package;

// output header
islands.header();

// set ptr to address of base class object
ptr = &islands;

// execute virtual function
// the compiler will know which version to execute!!
ptr->other_attractions();

// now set ptr to address of derived class objects
ptr = &package_1;
ptr->other_attractions();
ptr = &package_2;
ptr->other_attractions();
ptr = &package_3;
ptr->other_attractions();

// ** output name of mystery island
// ** set ptr to address of package_4
mystery_package.name();
ptr = &mystery_package;

// ** caribbean_isles::other_attractions executes
ptr->other_attractions();

return(0);
}
```

An object of type saba is given the name mystery_package. After the attractions of the other islands have been listed, the name of the mystery package island is output, ptr is set to point to an object of that type, and the function other_attractions() is executed. Here's the output of this program:

```
!!COME VISIT THE CARIBBEAN ISLANDS!!
White sandy beaches
Crystal clear water
No hassles - No worries - No cares

!!BAHAMAS!!
Fun-filled casinos
Action-packed water sports
Great rum punches
```

```
!!GRAND CAYMAN!!
Incredible scuba diving
Big time game fishing
Duty free shopping

!!ST THOMAS!!
Excellent shopping

!!MYSTERY ISLAND SABA!!
White sandy beaches
Crystal clear water
No hassles - No worries - No cares
```

As you can see, *the base virtual function turns out to be the default function which executes in the absense of an overridding function in the derived class*. At a future date, the other_attractions() function can be defined for the new derived class. Then, when the statement

```
ptr->other_attractions()
```

is executed

```
saba::other_attractions()
```

will be implemented instead of caribbean_isles::other_attractions().

17.4 Pure Virtual Functions and Abstract Classes

Pure virtual functions exist for scenarios that are the flip side of the coin of the previous section. There are circumstances in which the attributes of the virtual function in the base class are undefined. A pure virtual function is created in these circumstances.

- **Pure virtual functions are used simply as a *place holder* for functions that are *expected* to be derived from the base class in the future.**

- **Pure virtual functions have no definition in the base class; they are initialized to 0.**

- **Any class derived from a pure virtual function will be required to provide its own implementation of that function.**

The use of pure virtual functions is illustrated in test17_3.cpp:

```
// test17_3.cpp

#include <iostream.h>

// caribbean_isles is the base class
class caribbean_isles
    {
    public:

    // ** the header is output seperately
    void header(void)
        {cout << "!!COME VISIT THE CARRIBBEAN ISLANDS!! \n\n";}

    // attributes of other_attractions either do not exist,
    // or are simply a place holder.
    // therefore, we define it as a pure virtual function
    virtual void other_attractions(void) = 0;
    };
```

As you can see, the virtual function other_attractions() in the base class is initialized to 0. This is a pure virtual function.

■ *Declaring a pure virtual function results in each class that is derived from it being forced to provide its own implementation for that function.*

Let's continue with the program:

```
// bahamas, grand_cayman and st_thomas are derived from
// caribbean_isles.
class bahamas : public caribbean_isles
    {
    public:

    // ** notice same function name, no keyword virtual
    void other_attractions(void)
        {
        cout << "!!BAHAMAS!! \n";
        cout << "Fun-filled casinos \n";
        cout << "Action-packed water sports \n";
        cout << "Great rum punches \n\n";
        }
    };

class grand_cayman : public caribbean_isles
    {
    public:

    // ** notice same function name, no keyword virtual
    void other_attractions(void)
        {
        cout << "!!GRAND CAYMAN!! \n";
```

```
    cout << "Incredible scuba diving \n";
    cout << "Big time game fishing \n";
    cout << "Duty free shopping \n\n";
    }
};

class st_thomas : public caribbean_isles
    {
    public:

    // ** notice same function name, no keyword virtual
    void other_attractions(void)
        {
        cout << "!!ST THOMAS!! \n";
        cout << "Excellent shopping \n\n";
        }
    };
```

Now take a look at first few lines inside main().

```
main(void)
{
    // ** declare ptr only to caribbean_isles class
    // ** we can not create an object of a class type that has
    // ** a pure virtual function.
    caribbean_isles *ptr;
```

As you can see, an object for the base class is not declared. This is because

- *A base class that has a pure virtual function is said to be abstract.*

- **You cannot declare objects for abstract classes.**

- **It is permissable to declare pointers to classes that contain pure virtual functions. This is necessary in order to implement run-time polymorphism.**

Here's the remainder of the code:

```
    // declare objects for derived classes
    bahamas package_1;
    grand_cayman package_2;
    st_thomas package_3;

    // ** we output header() function of the base class,
    // ** but as an element of the derived class.
    package_1.header();

    // ** set ptr to object of derived class
    ptr = &package_1;
```

```
// execute virtual function
// the compiler will know which version to execute!!
ptr->other_attractions();
ptr = &package_2;
ptr->other_attractions();
ptr = &package_3;
ptr->other_attractions();

    return(0);
}
```

There are no further changes to the remainder of the code.

If we forgot to provide an implementation for the virtual function inside one of the derived classes, say, st_thomas, the compiler would issue the following error message:

```
Error:  Pure function 'caribbean_isles::other_attractions()'
        not overridden in 'st_thomas'
```

Therefore,

- **Pure virtual functions can be used as a safety mechanism inside programs where it is necessary for derived classes to provide their own version of the base virtual function.**

17.5 REVIEW

In this chapter, we wrapped up our discussion on virtual functions. We learned:

- Just how easy it is to incorporate new virtual functions into a program or delete outdated ones, based upon current needs.

- That a base virtual function is invoked in those instances where a derived class fails to provide an implementation for it.

- That pure virtual functions force the programmer to provide an implementation of the virtual function inside the derived class.

- That classes which contain pure virtual functions are called abstract classes. Objects of this type cannot be declared, only pointers to them. The virtual function inside an abstract class is used as a place holder for classes that will be derived from it.

Chapter 4

Operator Overloading

18.1 INTRODUCTION

In this chapter, we will describe an unusual and interesting feature of C++ called *operator overloading*.

- **Operator overloading allows you to change the meaning of operators such as +, -, *, /, and others.**

If you take the time to think through the reasons to overload operators, then you will see how this can be a very powerful tool. On the other hand, indiscriminate use of overloaded operators can result in a debugging nightmare. Keep this in mind as you proceed with the remainder of the chapter.

18.2 OPERATOR OVERLOADING IS NOTHING UNUSUAL

Take a look at the following six line program:

```
//    test18_1.cpp

#include <iostream.h>

main(void)
{
    cout << "Notice the use of the << operator!! \n";
}
```

Compiling and running this program will result in the following output:

```
Notice the use of the << operator!!
```

There are no mysteries here. Now take a look at test18_2.cpp, in which the << operator is used in the context of a left shift operator:

```
//    test18_2.cpp

#include <iostream.h>

main(void)
{
    int a = 2;
    cout << "a is " << a << "\n";

    // shift a left by 12 bits
    a = a << 12 ;
    cout << "a is " << a << "\n";
}
```

Compiling and running this program will result in the following output:

```
a is 2
a is 8192
```

What is interesting in this program is the use of the << operator. In the first instance, it is used as a *put to* operator. In the second program, the following statement

```
a = a << 12;
```

implies its use as the left shift operator. a is shifted left 12 bits, and so the value stored in a is output as 8192, instead of 2.

What you just encountered is an example of operator overloading. Operator overloading is a feature provided by C++ that allows you to change the meaning of operators. In the first example, the operator << is used as a *put to* operator. In the second example, it is used as a left shift operator, as well as a *put to* operator.

Operator overloading is an interesting concept, but you will be suprised to realize that it has existed all along, perhaps without your knowing about it. For example, you can add two integers using the + operator:

```
a = 5 + 2;
```

and you can add two floats using the same operator:

```
a = 5.5 + 2.8;
```

You are using the same operator to perform the same function on two different data types. The + operator is overloaded to perform addition on two integer types in the first instance and addition of two float types in the second.

Here's another example. The * operator is used to multiply two data types:

```
a = a * b;
```

However, the * operator can also be used to specifiy a pointer type when it is declared:

```
int *ptr;
```

The above statement declares ptr as a pointer to an integer type. The * operator can also be used to dereference a pointer variable, in order to manipulate the contents of what is stored at the location in memory that ptr is pointing to:

```
*ptr = 5;
```

The above statement sets the contents of the location in memory stored in ptr to 5. This is another instance of operator overloading.

18.3 SYNTAX OF OPERATOR OVERLOADING

Take a look at the following short program:

```
//    test18_3.cpp

#include <iostream.h>

class assign
    {
    public:
    int a;
    };

assign object_1, object_2;

main(void)
{
    object_1.a = 5;
    object_2 = object_1;

    cout << "object_2.a is " << object_2.a << "\n";
```

```
}
```

Compiling and running this program result in the following output:

```
object2.a is 5
```

This program demonstrates nothing but the simple assignment of an integer value to a class member, and then cout is used to display this value to your screen. Now take a look at the following program, which illustrates operator overloading. We will be overloading the assignment operator (=).

```
//    test18_4.cpp

#include <iostream.h>

class assign
    {
    public:
    int a;

    // ** notice overloaded function syntax:
    void operator=(assign var1);
    };

// overloaded operator function returns no value (type void)
// it takes an object of type assign as an argument
// it follows the usual function definition rules
void assign::operator=(assign var1)
{
    a = 2 + var1.a;
}

// object_1 and object_2 are objects of type assign
assign object_1, object_2;

main(void)
{
    // class member a of object_1 is assigned the value of 5
    object_1.a = 5;

    // object_2 is set equal to object_1
    object_2 = object_1;
    cout << "object_2.a is " << object_2.a << "\n";
}
```

Compiling and running this program will result in the following output:

```
object_2.a is 7
```

Interesting output, wouldn't you say? Under normal circumstances, object_2.a should have been 5, not 7, since object_2 is set equal to object_1, and object_1.a was previously set to 5. Well, the reason for this unusual output is that the operator = was *overloaded* to set the operand on the left equal to the operand on the right plus 2. That is why object_2.a was set equal to 7, instead of 5. Let's step through this program and understand what happened. Take a look at the declaration of the class assign:

```
class assign
    {
    public:
    int a;

    // ** notice overloaded function syntax:
    void operator=(assign var1);
    };
```

Notice the syntax for the member function assign():

```
    void operator=(assign var1);
```

This statement declares the existence of an overloaded operator function. It is a member function of the class assign. The operator that will be overloaded is the assignment operator =. This function will return no value, and it takes an object of type assign as an argument. This function could just as well have been declared as follows:

```
    assign operator=(void);
```

This would imply that it returns an object of type assign, and takes no arguments. Or, it could have been declared as:

```
    int operator=(char);
```

or with any other valid return or argument type. In our example, it is declared as:

```
    void operator=(assign var1);
```

The definition of the class member function operator=() follows:

```
void assign::operator=(assign var1)
{
    a = 2 + var1.a;
}
```

The object on the left of the operator is assigned to the object on the right. The a class member inside the function belongs to object_2. The definition of this function agrees with the function prototype in the class declaration. The function returns no value, it is a member of the class assign (shown by the scope resolution operator ::, which precedes the function name assign::operator=), it overloads the operator =, and it takes an object of type assign as an argument.

The function itself is only one line. It receives class object1 as a parameter and adds 2 to its object_2.a member. It assigns the resulting value to the class member a, and then returns back to main().

Inside main(), object_2 is assigned to object_1. This is a valid assignment, since both objects are of the same class type. Finally, the contents of object_2.a are output.

The reason for the unusual result is that the operator = has been overloaded for all objects that belong to the class of which the overloaded function is a member. Let's go over this concept in greater detail.

object_1 and object_2 are objects of type assign. The operator function = is a class member of assign. The rule is:

- **Each time an overloaded operator (=) is encountered or called to perform an operation on class objects that belong to the class type for which an overloaded function definition exists, the overloaded function definition will be substituted instead of the usual operation.**

(Friend function definitions can also be substituted, and these will be discussed later on in the chapter.)

Now take another look at the code for main().

```
assign object_1, object_2;

main(void)
{
    // class member a of object_1 is assigned the value of 5
    object_1.a = 5;

    // object_2 is set equal to object_1
    object_2 = object_1;
    cout << "object_2.a is " << object_2.a << "\n";
}
```

object_1 and object_2 are declared as objects of type assign. Inside main(), class member a of assign is set to 5. Next, object_2 is assigned to object_1. However, the operator = was previously declared as a member function of the class assign. Since object_1 and object_2 are objects of the same type, the compiler implements the code for that particular overloaded operator.

Before trying to understand what happens inside the function itself, you should note that in the first assignment statement

```
object_1.a = 5;
```

5 was, in fact, assigned to object_1, and 2 was not added to it. The reason for this is that

- **Both operands on the left and the right of the overloaded operator must belong to the same class that the overloaded operator (or friend function) belongs to, in order for the code for the overloaded operator to be executed.**

The operand on the right is a constant, not a member of the class object assign, hence the regular assignment operation is implemented. What this implies is that operators preserve their existing functionality in the absence of the above mentioned conditions. (In the case of unary operators, i.e., those that operate on one operand only, e.g., ++ and --, the overloaded operator will always be called, given that the operand belongs to the same class. These will be discussed later on in the chapter.)

Now take another look at the code for the overloaded operator function:

```
void assign::operator=(assign var1)
{
    a = 2 + var1.a;
}
```

As you can see, an argument called var1 is accepted by assign. This is the template for an object of type assign. 2 is added to the a member of this object, and the result is assigned to the a member of the second object. You should be wondering by now exactly which object is being added to, and which object is being assigned to. The answer is that the operand on the right of the operator is passed as the explicit argument to the function. Hence, in the statement

```
object_2 = object_1;
```

the argument that is passed to the overloaded operator as the explicit argument var1 is object_1. The object on the left of the operator is assigned to. The a class member inside the function itself belongs to object_2. (This particular mechanism will be discussed in greater detail shortly.) That is why the contents of object_2.a are changed from 5 to 7.

Meanwhile, the contents of object_1.a remain unchanged. We will modify test18_4.cpp to demonstrate just that.

```
//    test18_5.cpp

#include <iostream.h>

class assign
   {
   public:
   int a;

   // ** notice overloaded function syntax:
   void operator=(assign var1);
   };

// overloaded operator function returns no value
// it takes an object of type assign as an argument
// it follows the usual function definition rules
void assign::operator=(assign var1)
{
   a = 2 + var1.a;
}

// object_1 and object_2 are objects of type assign
assign object_1, object_2;

main(void)
{
   // class member a of object_1 is assigned the value of 5
   object_1.a = 5;

   // object_2 is set equal to object_1
   object_2 = object_1;
   cout << "object_2.a is " << object_2.a << "\n";
   cout << "object_1.a is " << object_1.a << "\n";
}
```

Compiling and running this program result in the following output:

```
object_2.a is 7
object_1.a is 5
```

The output should make sense. The operand on the right remains unchanged through the whole process.

18.4 Getting Carried Away With Operator Overloading

Test18_5.cpp will now be modified to demonstrate an instance where we get a little bit carried away with the concept just explained, and want to play tricks with your mind. Take a look at the following code:

```
//     test18_6.cpp

#include <iostream.h>

class assign
    {
    public:
    int a;

    // ** notice operator changed from = to +:
    void operator+(assign var1);
    };

// overloaded operator function returns object of type assign
// it takes an object of type assign as an argument
// it follows the usual function definition rules

void assign::operator+(assign var1)
{
    a = 2 + var1.a;
}

// object_1 and object_2 are objects of type assign
assign object_1, object_2;

main(void)
{
    // class member a of object_1 is assigned the value of 5
    object_1.a = 5;

    // ** the '+' actually performs an '='!!!!
    object_2 + object_1;
    cout << "object_2.a is " << object_2.a << "\n";
}
```

Two lines of code that you should pay special attention to are:

```
void operator+(assign var1);
```

and

```
object_2 + object_1;
```

In the first statement, the operator + is overloaded. In the second statement, object_2 is added to object_1, and is not assigned to anything. Compiling and running this program result in the following output:

```
object_2.a is 5
```

If the operator + was not overloaded, the statement

```
object_2 + object_1;
```

would have resulted in an unfriendly compiler error message. However, no errors are generated because

```
object_2 + object_1;
```

results in exactly the same sequence of operations that occurred when the code looked like this:

```
object_2 = object_1;
```

For those of us of who inherit the code of programmers who inadvertently changed the meaning of operators, statements such as

```
object_2 + object_1;
```

can result in acute cases of confusion, headache, frustration, and insomnia. Hence, a word of advise from us. Please don't overload operators to mean something that goes against the grain of their original meaning. Don't overload a + operator to mean a -, a * to mean a /, and so on. Do what you have to do, but think things through before you proceed. Don't play tricks with other people's minds; you may end up playing a trick on yourself!

18.5 OVERLOADED OPERATORS ARE SIMPLY FUNCTION CALLS

■ **An overloaded operator function syntax is simply an alternate form of a function call.**

Take a look at the following code. The function name operator() has been abbreviated to op().

```
//    test18_7.cpp

#include <iostream.h>

class assign
    {
    public:
    int a;

    // ** notice that op is now a regular function
```

```
    // ** and it returns an object of type assign
    assign op(assign var1);
    };

assign object_1, object_2;

// op() is a regular function
// it returns an object of type assign
// it takes an object of type assign as a parameter
assign assign::op(assign var1)
{
    a = 2 + var1.a;
    object_2 = object_1;

    cout << "object_2.a in op() function is "
         << object_2.a << "\n";

    return var1;
}

main(void)
{
    // class member a of object_1 is assigned the value of 5
    object_1.a = 5;

    // object_1.op() is executed
    // the return value is assigned to object_2
    object_2 = object_1.op(object_1);

    cout << "object_2.a is " << object_2.a << "\n";
}
```

Compiling and running this program will result in the following output:

```
object_2.a in op() function is 7
object_2.a is 5
```

The function op() is now a regular member function of the class assign(). object_1 and object_2 are declared as objects of type assign. Inside main(), the following statement

```
object_2 = object_1.op(object_1);
```

results in the function object_1.op() being called, object_1 is passed as a parameter to it. Inside the function, 2 is added to a class member of object_1, and assigned to object_2 in the statement

```
object_2 = object_1;
```

Hence, object_2.a in op() gets set to 7. However, object_1.a remains unchanged, and this is the value sent back to main(). object_2 is assigned this value, and object_2.a is now once again set to 5.

As you are aware, the contents of variables inside functions can be manipulated or changed only through pointers (unless you are passing an array to the function or global variables). This is because copies of parameters are passed to functions, not the actual values. Here's a short program that illustrates this point:

```
//     test18_8.cpp

#include <iostream.h>

class assign
    {
    public:
    int a;

    // ** notice that op is now a regular function
    assign op(assign *object_1);
    };

assign object_1, object_2, *ptr;

// op() is a regular function
// it returns an object of type assign
// it takes a pointer to an object of type assign as a parameter
assign assign::op(assign *ptr)
{
    // modify contents of what ptr is pointing to
    // ptr is pointing to object_1.a
    ptr->a = 2 + ptr->a;

    // return object_1
    return object_1;
}

main(void)
{
    // class member a of object_1 is assigned the value of 5
    object_1.a = 5;

    // set ptr to location in memory of object_1
    ptr = &object_1;

    // object_2 is set equal to return value of op()
    // this return value is an object of type assign
    object_2 = object_1.op(ptr);

    cout << "object_2.a is " << object_2.a << "\n";
}
```

Compiling and running this program will result in the following output:

object_2.a is 7

This time a pointer to object_1 is sent to the function op():

assign op(assign *object_1);

ptr is set to the location in memory of object_1, and then a call to op() is initiated.

Inside op(), the actual contents of object_1 are modified, via ptr:

ptr->a = 2 + ptr->a;

A member of object_1 is accessed via the -> operator. The dot (.) operator could also have been used as follows:

ptr.a = 2 + ptr.a;

The modified contents of object_1 are sent back to main(), and object_2 is assigned to this return value. Hence, object_2.a outputs as 7.

Now here's the trick question. Which version do you think looks cleaner and more natural? The one that uses pointers:

```
//    test18_8.cpp

#include <iostream.h>

class assign
    {
    public:
    int a;

    // ** notice that op is now a regular function
    assign op(assign *object_1);
    };

assign object_1, object_2, *ptr;

// op() is a regular function
// it returns an object of type assign
// it takes a pointer to an object of type assign as a parameter
assign assign::op(assign *ptr)
{
    // modify contents of what ptr is pointing to
    // ptr is pointing to object_1.a
    ptr->a = 2 + ptr->a;

    // return object_1
    return object_1;
}
```

```
main(void)
{
    // class member a of object_1 is assigned the value of 5
    object_1.a = 5;

    // set ptr to location in memory of object_1
    ptr = &object_1;

    // object_2 is set equal to return value of op()
    // this return value is an object of type assign
    object_2 = object_1.op(ptr);

    cout << "object_2.a is " << object_2.a << "\n";
}
```

or the one that uses operator overloading:

```
//    test18_4.cpp
#include <iostream.h>

class assign
    {
    public:
    int a;
    // ** notice overloaded function syntax:
    void operator=(assign var1);
    };

// overloaded operator function returns no value
// it takes an object of type assign as an argument
// it follows the usual function definition rules
void assign::operator=(assign var1)
{
    a = 2 + var1.a;
}

// object_1 and object_2 are objects of type assign
assign object_1, object_2;

main(void)
{
    // class member a of object_1 is assigned the value of 5
    object_1.a = 5;

    // object_2 is set equal to object_1
    object_2 = object_1;
    cout << "object_2.a is " << object_2.a << "\n";
}
```

If you prefer the first version, then you probably don't feel comfortable with the syntax of overloaded operator calls. We recommend that you refrain from using overloaded operators until you feel more comfortable with the concept and syntax.

If you prefer the second version, then you are well on your way to adopting yet another powerful feature of C++.

18.6 ADVANTAGES OF OPERATOR OVERLOADING

■ **One of the major advantages of operator overloading is that it allows you to use the same operators on user-defined data types as are used on built-in data types.**

You are used to expressions such as

```
a = a + b;
a = a * b;
```

but without operator overloading, the statements

```
object_1 = object_1 + object_2;
object_1 = object_1 * object_2;
```

would be invalid, given that `object_1` and `object_2` are user-defined data types. Operator overloading affords a more natural way for the expression of such statements. As another example, a concatenation of two strings would be expressed intuitively as follows:

```
"This is a " + "concatenation of 2 strings.";
```

The above statement would not compile properly without operator overloading.

18.7 DISADVANTAGES OF OPERATOR OVERLOADING

■ **The major disadvantage of operator overloading is the possibility that the meaning of operators can become hidden inside obscure code.**

The programmer may not understand why an operator such as + is not performing the function that he/she expects it to. The programmer is bound to experience feelings of inadequacy (since he/she does not understand the code), frustration, insomnia, and emotional distress.

18.8 REVIEW

In this chapter, we explained how operator overloading works, and why it can be a powerful or destructive tool. In particular, we learned that:

- We have been inadvertently overloading operators such as << and * all along; it is nothing new.

- This mechanism can be used to change the meaning of most operators provided by C++.

- Overloaded operator functions must be class members or friend functions.

- Overloaded operator functions are nothing more than an alternate form of a function call.

- The syntax for an overloaded function is as follows:

```
type operator#(argument_list);
```

  where *type* is the return type of the function. This can be type void or any other valid data type; # is the operator that is being overloaded; *argument_list* is the list of arguments, if any, which are sent to the overloaded function.

- Overloaded operators allow a more natural way to express the relationship between two user-defined data types.

- Overloaded operators can be a programmer's nightmare if their use results in obscure and impenetrable code.

Operator Overloading, this and friend

19.1 INTRODUCTION

In this chapter, we will introduce a pointer called this (yes, it really is called this!). This pointer (no pun intended) is an integral part of the mechanism that allows operator overloading. Use of friend functions will also be illustrated. Friends can be used instead of class members to overload operators.

19.2 BINARY AND UNARY OVERLOADED OPERATORS

A binary operator is one that works on two objects. For example, + is a binary operator, because you have to add something to something in order for it to work. A unary operator is one that works on one object only. For example, ++ is a unary operator; something++ results in something being incremented by 1.

Tables 19.1 and 19.2 list operators that cannot and can be overloaded, respectively.

Table 19.1 Operators That Cannot Be Overloaded

Operator	Function
,	comma
.	member
->	class or structure pointer
?:	ternary
sizeof	obtain size in bytes

Table 19.2 Operators That Can Be Overloaded

Operator	Function
++	increment
--	decrement
!	not
~	complement
+	add
-	minus
*	multiply
/	divide
%	modulus
()	function call
[]	array subscript
new	free store allocator
delete	free store deallocator
=	assign
+=	add and assign
-=	subtract and assign
*=	multiply and assign
/=	divide and assign
&	bitwise and
|	bitwise or
^	bitwise exclusive-or
||	logical or
&&	logical and
<	less than
<=	less than or equal to
>	greater than
>=	greater than or equal to
<<	left shift
>>	right shift
|=	or and assign
^=	exclusive-or and assign
&=	and and assign
<<=	left shift and assign
>>=	right shift and assign
==	logical equal
!=	not equal

19.3 Restrictions on Overloaded Operators

- You cannot make up your own operator. You can overload existing operators only.

- Operator overloading works when applied to class objects only.

- You cannot change the precedence or associativity of the original operators.

- You cannot change a binary operator to work with a single object.

- You cannot change a unary operator to work with two objects.

- Prefix and postfix application of the operators ++ and -- cannot be distinguished.

- You cannot overload an operator that works exclusively with pointers.

19.4 Expression Syntax of Overloaded Operators

We would like to bring your attention to the fourth and fifth restrictions from the previous section. These restrictions state that **you must respect the general form of syntax that is associated with a particular operator; that is, you cannot change its basic template.** Take a look at the following program:

```
//    test19_1.cpp

#include <iostream.h>

class assign
   {
   public:
   int a;

   // ** notice overloaded function syntax:
   void operator/(assign var1);
   };

// overloaded operator function returns type void (i.e. nothing)
// it takes an object of type assign as an argument
// it follows the usual function definition rules
void assign::operator/(assign var1)
{
   a = var1.a / 5;
}
```

```
// object_1 and object_2 are objects of type assign
assign object_1, object_2;

main(void)
{
    // class member a of object_1 is assigned the value of 5
    object_1.a = 15;
    object_2.a = 10;

    // The divide operator is treated as a unary operator
    object_2 / ;

    cout << "object_1.a is " << object_1.a << "\n";
    cout << "object_2.a is " << object_2.a << "\n";
}
```

Notice the statement:

```
object_2 / ;
```

As you can see, an attempt is made to use the division operator, which is binary, on a single object. Compiling this program results in the following error message:

```
Error:   Expression syntax
```

Now take a look at this program, which also overloads the divide operator but uses two objects instead of one.

```
//     test19_2.cpp

#include <iostream.h>

class assign
    {
    public:
    int a;

    // ** notice overloaded function syntax:
    void operator/(assign var1);
    };

// overloaded operator function returns type void
// it takes an object of type assign as an argument
// it follows the usual function definition rules
void assign::operator/(assign var1)
{
    a = var1.a / 5;
}
// object_1 and object_2 are objects of type assign
assign object_1, object_2;
```

```
main(void)
{
   object_1.a = 15;
   object_2.a = 10;

   cout << "object_2.a is " << object_2.a << "\n";

   // object_2 is divided by object_1
   object_2 7 object_1;

   cout << "object_1.a is " << object_1.a << "\n";
   cout << "object_2.a is " << object_2.a << "\n";
}
```

Compiling and running this program will result in the following output:

```
object_2.a is 10
object_1.a is 15
object_2.a is 3
```

object_1.a and object_2.a are initially set to 15 and 10, respectively. The division (/) operator is overloaded. object_2 is divided by object_1. The statement

```
a = var1.a / 5;
```

can be decoded as follows:

```
object_2.a = object_1.a / 5;
```

which is equal to

```
object_2.a = 15 / 5;
```

and so object_2.a is equal to 3. The output statements should now make sense. The contents of object_1.a remain unchanged. The contents of object_2.a are set to 3.

In the previous chapter, we had mentioned with reference to statements containing overloaded operators:

- **The operator on the right of the operand is sent as an explicit argument to the calling overloaded operator function.**

- **The operand on the left is implicitly sent to the calling function.**

In this chapter, this concept will be elaborated on, so that you can understand how this mechanism works. Take another look at the function definition:

```
void assign::operator/(assign var1)
{
    a = var1.a / 5;
}
```

Based on what has just been said, var1 will contain the value assigned to object_1, since object_1 is to the right of the overloaded operator. This is the explicit argument sent to the calling function.

A pointer to the left operand is implicitly passed to operator/(). Hence, the variable a in the statement

```
    a = var1.a / 5;
```

belongs to object_2. A pointer to object_2 is implicitly passed to the overloaded function. But exactly how does this occur? The answer is through a pointer that Mr. Stroustrup chose to call the this pointer.

19.5 THE THIS POINTER

- **Each time a member function is invoked, it is passed a pointer to the object that invoked it. The name of this pointer is this.**

- **This pointer is invisible to us because it is passed automatically or implicitly.**

- **The syntax of this pointer is similar to other pointer syntax. The only difference is that it is never declared, since its existence is automatic.**

And now, just to prove that a pointer to the operand on the left side of the overloaded operator is implicitly passed to the calling function through this pointer, here's a modified version of test19_2.cpp.

```
//    test19_3.cpp

#include <iostream.h>

class assign
    {
    public:
    int a;

    // ** notice overloaded function syntax:
    void operator/(assign var1);
    };
```

```
// overloaded operator function returns no value
// it takes an object of type assign as an argument
// it follows the usual function definition rules
void assign::operator/(assign var1)
{
    cout << "this->a is " << this->a << "\n";
    a = var1.a / 5;
}

// object_1 and object_2 are objects of type assign
assign object_1, object_2;

main(void)
{
    object_1.a = 15;
    object_2.a = 10;

    // ** object_2 is divided by object_1
    object_2 / object_1;

    cout << "object_1.a is " << object_1.a << "\n";
    cout << "object_2.a is " << object_2.a << "\n";
}
```

Compiling and running this program will give the following output:

```
this->a is 10
object_1.a is 15
object_2.a is 3
```

As you can see, `this->a` contains the value 10, which was assigned to `object_2.a` in `main()`. The statement

```
a = var1.a / 5;
```

can be decoded as follows:

```
object_2.a = object_1.a / 5;
```

which is equal to

```
object_2.a = 15 / 5;
```

and so `object_2.a` is set equal to 3. The output statements should now be clear.

Let's switch the values of `object_1` and `object_2` inside `main()`, and see how the value of the `this` pointer is affected. Here's the code:

```
//    test19_4.cpp
```

```
#include <iostream.h>

class assign
    {
    public:
    int a;

    // ** notice overloaded function syntax:
    void operator/(assign var1);
    };

// overloaded operator function returns object of type assign
// it takes an object of type assign as an argument
// it follows the usual function definition rules
void assign::operator/(assign var1)
{
    cout << "this->a is " << this->a << "\n";
    a = var1.a / 5;
}

// object_1 and object_2 are objects of type assign
assign object_1, object_2;

main(void)
{
    object_1.a = 15;
    object_2.a = 10;

    cout << "object_2.a is " << object_2.a << "\n";

    // object_1 is divided by object_2
    object_1 7 object_2;

    cout << "object_1.a is " << object_1.a << "\n";
    cout << "object_2.a is " << object_2.a << "\n";
}
```

Compiling and running this program will result in the following output:

```
object_2.a is 10
this->a is 15
object_1.a is 2
object_2.a is 10
```

The statement

```
a = var1.a / 5;
```

can be decoded as follows:

```
object_1.a = object_2.a / 5;
```

which is equal to

```
object_1.a = 10 / 5;
```

and so `object_1.a` is set equal to 2, and `object_2.a` remains unchanged.
The output should now be self-explanatory.

And now, to reinforce what you have just learned, here's another
program that illustrates how operator overloading works. This time the
* operator will be overloaded.

```
//     test19_5.cpp
#include <iostream.h>

class assign
    {
    public:
    int a;

    // ** notice return value of overloaded function
    int operator*(assign var1);
    };

// overloaded operator function returns integer
// it takes an object of type assign as an argument
// it follows the usual function definition rules
int assign::operator*(assign var1)
{
    cout << "this->a is " << this->a << "\n";
    a = this->a * var1.a;
    return a;
}

// object_1, object_2 and object_3 are objects of type assign
assign object_1, object_2, object_3;

main(void)
{
    object_1.a = 15;
    object_2.a = 10;

    // object_3.a receives the return value
    object_3.a = object_2 * object_1;

    cout << "object_1.a is " << object_1.a << "\n";
    cout << "object_2.a is " << object_2.a << "\n";
    cout << "object_3.a is " << object_3.a << "\n";
}
```

Notice that this time the overloaded function returns an `int`, instead
of an object of type `assign`. Inside the function, a is returned, which is
a class member of `object_2`. Since an `int` type is being returned, `main()`

is modified to have an `int` type accept this value.

Compiling and running this program will result in the following output:

```
this->a is 10
object_1.a is 15
object_2.a is 150
object_3.a is 150
```

The statement

```
object_3.a = object_2 * object_1;
```

results in `object_2` being multiplied by `object_1`. The * operator is overloaded. Inside the overloaded function:

```
int assign::operator*(assign var1)
{
   cout << "this->a is " << this->a << "\n";
   a = this->a * var1.a;
   return a;
}
```

`object_1` is sent explicitly, and a pointer to `object_2` is sent implicitly. The variables `a` and `this->a` belong to `object_2` (they are to the left of the overloaded operator). Thus, the statement

```
a = this->a * var1.a;
```

can be decoded as follows:

```
object_2.a = 10 * 15;
```

Thus, the value of `object_1.a` remains unchanged, and `object_2.a` is returned via the statement:

```
return a;
```

and assigned to `object_3.a`:

```
object_3.a = object_2 * object_1;
```

The output should now be absolutely clear to you.

19.6 FRIEND FUNCTIONS

So far, member functions only have been used to illustrate how operator overloading works.

- **Friend functions to the class that contains the overloaded operator function definition can also be used with operator overloading.**

As you have seen, member functions that overload binary operators are passed only one argument, and a pointer to the argument is passed implicitly through the this pointer.

- **Overloaded unary operator function definitions require no arguments.**

- **In friend functions, overloaded unary operators take one argument, and binary operators take two arguments. Both arguments are passed explicitly.**

- **The** this **pointer cannot be used with friend functions, since it returns the location in memory of a class member for member functions only, and a friend function does not fall into this category.**

Take a look at test19_6.cpp, which illustrates the use of a friend function that overloads an operator:

```
//    test19_6.cpp

#include <iostream.h>

class assign
    {
    public:
    int a;

    // ** notice friend function
    friend int operator*(assign var1, assign var2);
    };

// overloaded operator function returns integer
// it takes two objects of type assign as arguments
// it follows the usual function definition rules
// operator* is a friend function, therefore there is no
// scope resolution operator for it.
int operator*(assign var_1, assign var_2)
{
    var_2.a = var_1.a * var_2.a;
```

```
    return var_2.a;
}

// object_1, object_2 and object_3 are objects of type assign
assign object_1, object_2, object_3;

main(void)
{
    object_1.a = 15;
    object_2.a = 10;

    // object_3.a receives the return value
    object_3.a = object_2 * object_1;

    cout << "object_1.a is " << object_1.a << "\n";
    cout << "object_2.a is " << object_2.a << "\n";
    cout << "object_3.a is " << object_3.a << "\n";
}
```

Take another look at the function definition:

```
int operator*(assign var_1, assign var_2)
{
    var_2.a = var_1.a * var_2.a;
    return var_2.a;
}
```

Notice that the name of the function is not preceded by a scope resolution operator. This makes sense because there is no scope to resolve, since this is a friend function. Also notice that both arguments are passed explicitly.

Compiling and running this program will result in the following output:

```
object_1.a is 15
object_2.a is 10
object_3.a is 150
```

Now take another look at the statement that calls the overloaded operator function:

```
    object_3.a = object_2 * object_1;
```

The object on the left of the overloaded operator *, i.e., object_2, is assigned to var1. The object on the right, i.e., object_1, is assigned to var2. Inside the function, the values of the objects themselves do not change, since copies of these objects are manipulated. The return value is assigned to object_3.a, and therefore 50 is output for this data type.

If the contents of object_1 or object_2 are to be modifed, these objects can be sent as references. Here's a program that illustrates how parameters can be sent by reference, instead of value:

```
//     test19_7.cpp

#include <iostream.h>

class assign
    {
    public:
    int a;

    // ** notice friend function
    friend int operator*(assign object_1, assign &object_2);
    };

// overloaded operator function returns integer
// it takes two objects of type assign as arguments
// it follows the usual function definition rules
// operator* is a friend function, therefore there is no
// scope resolution operator for it.
// var_2 is passed as a reference.
int operator*(assign var_1, assign &var_2)
{
    var_2.a = var_1.a * 5;
    var_2.a = var_1.a * var_2.a;
    return var_2.a;
}

// object_1, object_2 and object_3 are objects of type assign
assign object_1, object_2, object_3;

main(void)
{
    object_1.a = 15;
    object_2.a = 10;

    // object_3.a receives the return value
    object_3.a = object_2 * object_1;

    cout << "object_1.a is " << object_1.a << "\n";
    cout << "object_2.a is " << object_2.a << "\n";
    cout << "object_3.a is " << object_3.a << "\n";
}
```

Notice the function prototype for the overloaded friend function:

```
friend int operator*(assign var1, assign &var2);
```

As you can see, the first parameter is sent by value; that is, a copy of this variable is sent to the calling function. The second parameter is sent by reference (the & sign precedes the variable name).

Compiling and running this program will result in the following output:

```
object_1.a is 500
object_2.a is 10
object_3.a is 500
```

The statement

```
object_3.a = object_2 * object_1;
```

results in the overloaded operator function being called. Inside the function, var_1 is assigned the value of object_2 (10), since it is to the left of the overloaded operator, and var_2 is assigned the value of object_1 (15). The statement

```
var_2.a = var_1.a * 5;
```

is decoded as follows:

```
object_1.a = object_2.a * 5;
```

object_1.a is set to 10 * 5, which is equal to 50.

Since object_1 is passed as a reference, its actual value is also changed to 50. The statement

```
var_2.a = var_1.a * var_2.a;
```

is decoded as follows:

```
object_1.a = object_2.a * object_1.a;
```

which is equal to

```
object_1.a = 10 * 50;
```

and object_1.a is set equal to 500. The output should now make sense.

- **Friend functions make the code for overloaded operators easier to read, since all arguments sent are visible to the human eye.**

There are no implicit or hidden arguments involved. Whether you use class members or friend functions to overload operators is your prerogative. Regardless of your choice, remember that one day someone will probably inherit your code. Make sure your overloaded function code is not impossible to penetrate, comment liberally, and don't play tricks with people's minds.

19.7 REVIEW

In this chapter, we described some additional features of overloaded operators.

- The majority of existing operators can be overloaded.

- There are some restrictions with reference to the extent to which operators can be overloaded.

- A pointer to the object on the left of a binary overloaded operator is implicitly passed to the calling function via the this pointer.

- The object to the right of the overloaded operator is passed explicitly as a parameter to the calling function.

- Binary overloaded operators are passed one argument.

- Unary overloaded operators are passed no arguments.

- Friend functions can be used to overload operators as well. Friends require that all parameters be sent to the calling function explicitly.

C++ Preprocessor Directives

20.1 INTRODUCTION

In this chapter, C++ preprocessor directives will be described.

- **Preprocessor directives allow the inclusion of files, implement simple string replacement, expand macros, and perform conditional compilation.**

Some directives help us in debugging the source code as well. But first, let's understand what a preprocessor is.

20.2 THE C++ PREPROCESSOR

C++ comes with a standard library of functions, which are normally included with the standard C++ compiler package.

- **The preprocessor is a program that processes the source code of a program before it passes the source code on to the compiler.**

- **Preprocessor directives are preceded by the # symbol, and are called preprocessor control lines.**

Based on the control lines, the preprocessor performs one or more of the following functions:

- **Includes files.**

  Files are included when the following directive is encountered:

  `#include`

- **Replaces strings, and expands and/or undefines macros.**

  The above two functions are implemented when the following directives are encountered:

  ```
  #define
  #undef
  ```

- **Performs conditional compilation.**

  Conditional compilation is implemented through the following sets of control lines:

  ```
  #if
  #else
  #endif

  #if
  #elif
  #endif

  #ifdef
  #endif

  #ifndef
  #endif
  ```

- **Aids in debugging.**

  The following control line helps debugging:

  `#pragma`

  The following sections describe each of the directives.

20.3 INCLUDE FILES

We have been including the file <iostream.h> in all our programs. Let's take a look at what happens if this file is not included.

```
//    test20_1.cpp
main(void)
{
   cout << "Hi there! \n";
   printf ("Hi there again! \n");
}
```

Compiling this program will result in the following error messages:

```
Error:   Undefined symbol 'cout'
Error:   Function 'printf()' should have a prototype
```

Obviously, iostream.h has been included for good reason. Let's include the necessary files and recompile:

```
//    test20_2.cpp

// iostream.h is required for I/O
// stdio.h is required for printf()
#include <iostream.h>
#include <stdio.h>

main(void)
{
   cout << "Hi there! \n";
   printf ("Hi there again! \n");
}
```

Compiling and running this program will result in the following output:

```
Hi there!
Hi there again!
```

The #include directive causes the entire contents of the name of the file that follows the directive to be included in the compilation. The header file iostream.h contains the definition for cout, and stdio.h contains the definition for printf().

The #include directive can take three forms.

- #include <filename>

You should be familiar with this form. The name of the file inside angular brackets instructs the compiler to search for the file from the list of prearranged directories that are outside the current working directory.

- #include "filename"

This form instructs the compiler to search for the file inside the current working directory.

- #include "C:\DIRNAME\FILENAME"

This form instructs the compiler to search for the file inside the specified path. If it is not found in that directory, then the standard directories are searched.

Here's a short program that illustrates the form in which the path name is indicated.

```cpp
//    test20_3.cpp

// iostream.h is required for I/O
// stdio.h is required for printf()
#include <iostream.h>
#include <stdio.h>

#include "C:\WP51\fileone"

main(void)
{
   cout << "Hi there! \n";
   printf ("Hi there again! \n");
   cout << "a from fileone is " << a << "\n";
}
```

We happen to have a directory called WP51 in our computer. (As a matter of fact, this is where our word processor resides.) This is what fileone looks like:

```cpp
int a = 5;
```

That's right. fileone is only one line long. Normally, the file that is included is quite large. In fact, that's the whole point of include files. It helps break up a large source file into logical, manageable segments. Compiling and running this program result in the following output:

```
Hi there!
Hi there again!
a from fileone is 5
```

- **Although the preprocessor includes the file in the current source code, it is still the compiler's responsibility to check for syntax errors and the like.**

Unfriendly messages will be generated by the compiler if the file which is included does not compile properly. Suppose a file called filetwo is included, which looks like this:

```
int a = 5
```

Notice the missing semicolon. Now take a look at a program that includes filetwo:

```
//    test20_4.cpp

#include <iostream.h>
#include <stdio.h>
#include "C:\WP50\filetwo"

main(void)
{
    cout << "Hi there! \n";
    printf ("Hi there again! \n");
    cout << "a from filetwo is " << a << "\n";
}
```

Compiling this program results in five errors, the first one being:

```
Error:   Declaration syntax error
```

This is a slightly misleading error message, wouldn't you say? We will not list the remaining error messages, since they make no sense either. The lesson to be learned from this is

■ **Make sure that your #include files compile properly before you include them in your source code; otherwise you may have to face a debugging nightmare.**

20.4 SIMPLE STRING REPLACEMENT

■ **Simple string replacement occurs with the #define directive.**

Take a look at this short program, which illustrates the use of this control line:

```
//    test20_5.cpp

#include <iostream.h>

#define HELLO "Hi there! \n"

main(void)
```

```
{
    cout << HELLO ;
}
```

Compiling and running this program will result in the following output:

```
Hi there!
```

HELLO is replaced by the string Hi there! \n each time it is encountered in the source code. The statement

```
    cout << HELLO;
```

is replaced by

```
    cout << "Hi there! \n";
```

and that is why you see the output

```
Hi there!
```

on your screen.

Most programmers use all capital letters when they use the #define control line. It is a good convention to follow, since it clearly identifies the variables which are defined in your program.

20.5 MACROS WITHOUT ARGUMENTS

■ **Macro expansion is a form of string replacement.**

Arguments can be also be specified and these will be discussed in the next section. Take a look at the following program, which illustrates the expansion of a simple macro.

```
//    test20_6.cpp

#include <iostream.h>

#define SQUARE_TWO 2*2

main(void)
{
    int a;
    a = SQUARE_TWO;
    cout << "a is " << a << "\n";
}
```

In the line

```
#define SQUARE_TWO 2*2
```

`#define` is the control line, `SQUARE_TWO` is the macro template, and `2*2` is the macro expansion. This is a macro definition. Compiling this program results in the following output:

```
a is 4
```

This output is achieved because the statement

```
a = SQUARE_TWO;
```

is expanded to

```
a = 2 * 2;
```

which, of course, is equal to 4.

■ **Macro expansions are valuable in that they define string replacement inside a program in one location only.**

Suppose you have a 500 line program in which 2 is squared 60 times, the code for each instance being scattered throughout the program. Now suppose you need to change the application to have 2 multiplied by 8, instead of 2. All you would have to do is change one line of code, the macro definition, as follows:

```
#define SQUARE_TWO  2*8
```

and all subsequent references to `SQUARE_TWO` will be changed accordingly.

20.6 MACROS WITH ARGUMENTS

Here's a short program that expands a macro with an argument:

```
//    test20_7.cpp
#include <iostream.h>
#define ADD(X) (X + X)

main(void)
{
```

```
    int b;
    b = ADD(4);
    cout << "b is " << b << "\n";
}
```

The control line

```
#define ADD(X) (X + X)
```

is referenced in the following statement

```
    b = ADD(4);
```

which expands to

```
    b = 4 + 4;
```

Compiling and running this program will result in the following output:

```
b is 8
```

Take another look at the control line:

```
#define ADD(X) (X + X)
```

Notice that there is no space between the macro template and its parameter X. If there was a space in between, then the token that follows it would become part of the macro expansion. Take a look at test20_8.cpp, which illustrates this form of expansion.

```
//    test20_8.cpp

#include <iostream.h>

// notice space between macro name and parameter
#define ADD (X) (X + X)

main(void)
{
    int b;
    b = ADD(4);
    cout << "b is " << b << "\n";
}
```

Compiling this program gives the following error message:

```
Error:   Undefined symbol 'X'
```

The compiler does not understand that the 4 inside the parentheses is the parameter that is to be substituted when the string is expanded. The space acts as a delimiter of the macro template.

Now suppose we forgot to place the parentheses in the control line, as follows:

```
#define ADD(X) X + X
```

This ommission can be potentially dangerous, as is illustrated by the following program:

```
//    test20_9.cpp

#include <iostream.h>

// notice space between macro name and parameter
#define ADD(X) X + X

main(void)
{
    int b;

    // we multiply the result of the macro expansion by 5
    b = ADD(4) * 5;

    cout << "b is " << b << "\n";
}
```

Compiling and running this program will give the following output:

```
b is 24
```

The statement

```
    b = ADD(4) * 5;
```

was expanded as follows:

```
    b = 4 + 4 * 5;
```

and since multiplication takes precedence over addition, b was calculated as follows:

```
    b = 4 + (4 * 5);
```

However, what we wanted was this:

```
    b = (4 + 4) * 5
```

The expression was not evaluated as expected since the parentheses are missing. Make sure you don't forget them.

20.7 UNDEFINING MACROS

■ Macros that have been previously defined can be undefined with the **following control line:**

#undef

This control line will result in no string replacement. Take a look at test20_10.cpp, which illustrates its use:

```
//    test20_10.cpp

#include <iostream.h>

#define FOUR 4

main(void)
{
    int a = FOUR;
    cout << "a is " << a << "\n";

    #undef FOUR
    int b = FOUR;
    cout << "b is " << b << "\n";
}
```

Compiling this program results in the following error message:

```
Error:   Undefined symbol FOUR
```

This message is output for the following statement:

```
int b = FOUR;
```

This is because FOUR was undefined just before this statement. The compiler no longer substitutes 4 for FOUR.

The reason for undefining a macro would be so that macro names can be localized for those sections of code in which they are needed.

20.8 CONDITIONAL COMPILATION

- **Conditional compilation takes place when the following keywords are encountered in the source code:**

```
#if - #else - #endif
#if - #elif - #endif
#ifdef - #endif
#ifndef - #endif
```

We will discuss each in the following subsections.

20.8.1 #if **and** #endif

The #if keyword is followed by a constant expression, a block of code, and then the #endif keyword.

- **The block of code between #if and #endif is included in compilation only if the constant expression between the braces evaluates to TRUE, or a nonzero value.**

Take a look at test20_11.cpp, which illustrates its use:

```
//    test20_11.cpp

#include <iostream.h>
main(void)
{
    const int a = 5;
    const int b = 0;

    #if (a)
        cout << "a is TRUE, i.e., non-zero \n";
    #else
        cout << "a is FALSE i.e., zero \n";
    #endif

    #if (b)
        cout << "b is TRUE, i.e., non-zero \n";
    #else
        cout << "b is FALSE, i.e., zero \n";
    #endif

    cout << "This code is outside the blocks \n";
}
```

Compiling and running this program will give the following output:

```
a is TRUE, i.e., non-zero
b is FALSE i.e., zero
```
This code is outside the blocks

The output is self-explanatory. Note that it is necessary for a constant expression to be inside the test condition. An error message will be generated if it isn't, as is illustrated by test20_12.cpp:

```
//    test20_12.cpp

#include <iostream.h>

main(void)
{
    // a and b are declared as variables
    int a = 5;
    int b = 0;

    #if (a)
        cout << "a is TRUE, i.e., non-zero \n";
    #else
        cout << "a is FALSE i.e., zero \n";
    #endif

    #if (b)
        cout << "b is TRUE, i.e., non-zero \n";
    #else
        cout << "b is FALSE, i.e., zero \n";
    #endif


    cout << "This code is outside the blocks \n";
}
```

Compiling this program results in the following error message:

```
Error:   Constant expression required
```

The difference between the #if, #else, and #endif and the regular if, else, and endif control structures is that in the former case evaluation takes place before the program is compiled and run. You cannot have variables inside the test condition, since their value can change at run time.

20.8.2 #if, #elif, **and** #endif

■ **These control lines are equivalent to the** #if, #else, **and** #endif
  control lines just discussed.

They will not be elaborated on any further.

20.8.3 #ifdef **and** #endif

■ **The block of code between** #ifdef **and** #endif **is compiled only if the macro name that follows the directive has been previously defined.**

Take a look at test20_13.cpp:

```
//    test20_13.cpp

#include <iostream.h>

#define COMPILE

main(void)
{
    #ifdef COMPILE
        cout << "This code will be compiled \n";
    #endif
}
```

Compiling and running this program will result in the following output:

```
This code will be compiled
```

As you can see, the macro COMPILE is defined; hence, the code within these two control lines is compiled. If the #define statement in the previous program is commented out, the code within the control lines will not be compiled. test20_4.cpp illustrates this.

```
//    test20_14.cpp

#include <iostream.h>

// we comment out the macro definition of COMPILE
// #define COMPILE

main(void)
{
    #ifdef COMPILE
        cout << "This code will be compiled \n";
    #endif
}
```

Compiling this program results in no output, since the macro called COMPILE is not defined.

■ **This preprocessor feature can be used as a debugging aid.**

Debug statements can be inserted for a macro name, and then this name can be commented and uncommented, in order to exclude or include the debugging statements in the source code.

20.8.4 #ifndef **and** #endif

These control lines are the flip side of #ifdef and #endif statements.

■ **The block of code between #ifndef and #endif is included in the compilation only if the macro name is not defined.**

Here's a program that illustrates just that.

```
//    test20_15.cpp

#include <iostream.h>

#define  COMPILE

main(void)
{
    // the following code is compiled only if macro
    // is not defined
    #ifndef COMPILE
        cout << "This code will be compiled \n";
    #endif
}
```

Compiling and running this program will result in no output. This is because COMPILE is defined. There would have been output if the macro control line was commented out or deleted.

20.9 #PRAGMA

■ **This control line allows various instructions to be given to the compiler. The instructions are specific to implementations.**

Please refer to your compiler's documentation for the #pragma directives that exist for your compiler.

20.10 REVIEW

In this chapter, we discussed the preprocessor and its directives. We learned how to:

- Include files:

```
#include <fileone>
#include "fileone"
#include "c:\dir\fileone"
```

- Perform simple string replacement, by defining macros:

```
#define HELLO "hello"
```

The above statement will result in HELLO being replaced by hello every time it is encountered in the source code file.

- Undefine macros, so that string replacement does not take place:

```
#undef HELLO
```

- Define macros with arguments:

```
#define square(x) (x*x)
```

The above control line takes one argument, and expands it as indicated.

- Compile conditionally, through the following control lines:

#if, #else, and #endif

The code between the block is compiled only if the constant expression in the test condition evaluates to TRUE or a nonzero value.

These directives are equivalent to #if, #else, and #endif directives:

#if, #elif, and #endif

The code between the block is compiled only if the macro name that follows the directive has been previously defined:

#ifdef and #endif

The code between the control lines is compiled only if the macro name is not defined:

#ifndef and #endif

- How to use the #pragma directive, which issures instructions to the compiler. This directive is implementation dependent.

Appendix
A

Glossary of Terms

Abstract Classes.   A base class which has a member that is a pure virtual function. Abstract classes can be used only as base classes that are to be inherited by subsequent classes.

Binding. The occurence of the event in which the address of a procedure is given to the caller. See *Early Binding* and *Late Binding* as well.

C++. An object-oriented language developed by Bjarne Stroustrup in the mid 1980's, a successor of C.

Classes. A definition of an object which can contain members and access privileges of these members to specific functions or methods within the declaration.

Constructor. A method or function which automatically initializes objects when they are created. The C++ compiler calls constructors implicitly if an explicit definition is not supplied.

Data Hiding. A mechanism by which data for members declared as private is hidden from all functions except those that are declared within the class.

Destructor. A method or function used to deallocate memory that may have been allocated to objects through constructors. The C++ compiler calls destructors implicitly, if an explicit definition is not supplied.

Dynamic Binding. Late binding. The occurence of the determination of events that are to take place at the time that a program is run. The addresses of procedures or functions are determined at run-time. Late binding makes polymorphism possible.

Early Binding. The occurence of the determination of events that are to take place at the time that a program is compiled. The addresses of procedures or functions are determined at compile/link time.

Encapsulation. The mechanism by which data and functions that are allowed to manipulate this data are bound together within an object definition.

Extensibility. A feature which is provided by object-oriented languages which allows the extension of existing code without knowledge of (or need for) the existing source. Extension of code allows the creation of new objects from existing ones.

Friend Functions. A function within a class which is not a member of that class. However, it has full access to the private and protected members of that class.

Free Store Objects. Objects which are created dynamically by the operator new from the free store, or heap. Free store is the pool of unallocated memory that is provided to a program when it is run.

Information Hiding. See *Encapsulation*.

Inheritance. The property by which one class derives all data members and function definitions from one or more other classes (except private members), without having to re-state them. This allows the creation of new objects from existing ones, resulting in a logical hierarchy of objects.

Inline Functions. Member functions or methods which are defined within the class itself. The compiler compiles the code for inline functions at the time that the keyword inline is encountered. This results in a reduction of processing and function call overhead for the program.

Instance. The existence of a predefined object.

Late Binding. See *Dynamic Binding*.

Member Function. A method within a class. A method is nothing more than a function prototype within the declaration of a class. This function may or may not be inline (i.e. defined).

Method. See *Member Function*.

Multiple Inheritance. The feature by which one object inherits data and functions from two or more base classes. See also *Inheritance*.

Object. An instance or occurrence of a class.

Object Oriented. The term given to languages which allow the collection of individual blocks of code into hierarchies of classes, thereby allowing code re-use and code extension without redefinition.

Operator Overloading. A feature which allows the meaning of most unary and binary operators to be changed.

Polymorphism. The property by which virtual functions are invoked using pointers to base classes, resulting in each object within the hierarchy implementing a method specific to its own requirements.

Private. The feature which allows the encapsulation of data and functions within that class alone. Data and functions within an object are private by default. See also *Protected* and *Public*.

Privately Derived Class. Classes which are preceded by the keyword "private" at the time that they are derived from a base class. This results in public and protected members of the base becoming private for the derived. Private members of the base class continue to remain private to it.

Protected. The feature which allows the encapsulation of functions within that class and derived classes only. See also *Private* and *Public*.

Public. The feature which allows the accessibility of data elements and functions to derived classes and the remainder of the application.

Publicly Derived Classes. Classes which are preceded by the keyword "public" at the time that they are derived from a base class. This results in public and protected members of the base becoming public and protected for the derived. Private members of the base class continue to remain private to it.

Reusability. See *Object Oriented*.

This. An invisible identifier which automatically points to the object for which it exists, and exists for each instance of that object. It is passed implicitly to overloaded operator functions.

Virtual Function or Method. A virtual function is usually a group of functions which have identical names but different implementation. The appropriate function is invoked based on the address of the particular object that is pointed to at the time. Virtual functions are implemented with dynamic binding. See also *Dynamic Binding* and *Polymorphism*.

Appendix
B

C++ Syntax

Format Notation:

- Syntactic definitions will be followed by a colon.

- Alternatives will follow on the next line.

- Optional elements will be enclosed within angle brackets (<..>).

Declaration Syntax

```
declaration:
     <declaration_specifiers><declaration_list>

declaration_specifiers:
     storage_class_specifier
     type_specifer
     function_specifier

declaration_list:
     declaration

storage_class_specifiers:
     auto
     register
     static
     extern

type_specifiers:
     type_name
     class_specifier
     enum_specifier
     const
     volatile
```

```
function_specifiers:
      inline
      virtual
      friend

type_names:
      class_name
      typedef_name
      char
      short
      int
      long
      signed
      unsigned
      float
      double
      void

class_specifiers:
      class
      struct
      union

enum_specifiers:
      enum <identifier>{enum_list}

enum_list:
      identifier
      identifier = constant_expression
```

Expression Syntax

```
expression:
      primary_expression
      expression binary_operator expression
      expression_list

operators:
      =     *=    /=    %=    +=-   =     <<=   >>=
      &=    ^=    |=    +-          <<    >>    <
      <=    >     >=    ==    !=    &     ^     |
      &&    ||    ?=

primary_expression
      constant
      string
      this
      ::identifier
      ::operator_function_name
      name
```

```
name:
    identifier
    operator_function_name
    class_name::identifier
    class_name::operator_function_name
    class_name::class_name
    class_name::~class_name

allocation_expression:
    <::> new <expression_list> type_specifier <initializer>

deallocation_expression:
    <::> delete expression
```

Class Declaration Syntax

```
class_specifier:
    base_specifier { member_list }

base_specifier:
    class_name
    virtual <access_specifier> class_name
    friend class_name

member_list
    member_declaration <member_list>

access_specifiers:
    private
    public
    protected

member_declarations:
    <declaration_specifiers><member_list>
    function_definitions

member_list
    member_declaration <member_list>
    access_specifier:<member_list>

operator_function_name:
    operator operator

operators:
    +-          *     /     %     ^
    &     |     ~     !     =     <>
    +=-   =     *=    /=    %=    ^=
    &=    |=    <<    >>    <<=   >>=
    ==    !=    <=    >=    &&    ||
    ++--        ,-    >*-   >     ()
    []    new   delete      sizeof
```

Index